W. S. Fowler

First Certificate English

Book 1 Language and Composition

NELSON

Thomas Nelson and Sons Ltd
36 Park Street London W1
P.O. Box 27 Lusaka
P.O. Box 18123 Nairobi
P.O. Box 21149 Dar es Salaam
77 Coffee Street San Fernando Trinidad

Thomas Nelson (Australia) Ltd
19-39 Jeffcott Street,
West Melbourne, Victoria 3003

Thomas Nelson and Sons (Canada) Ltd
81 Curlew Drive Don Mills Ontario

Thomas Nelson (Nigeria) Ltd
P.O. Box 336 Apapa Lagos

© W. S. Fowler 1973
First published 1973
Reprinted 1974 (twice), 1975 (twice)
17 555091 3

Recorded material for this book is available from the publishers and
from The Tutor Tape Company Ltd., 102 Great Russell Street,
London WC1B 3LE.

Printed in Hong Kong by
Dai Nippon Printing Co. (H.K.) Ltd.

Contents

Section Four – Composition

Introduction

Students preparing for the University of Cambridge First Certificate in English and comparable examinations have reached this level by a variety of paths and methods and so their strengths and weaknesses are also bound to vary. However, it must be remembered that such examinations are primarily tests of students' ability to write in English. Few students entering these classes have much experience in writing composition in English without guidance.

The object of this book is therefore to revise the main structures students have already met at an earlier stage in such a way that at the same time they can develop the skills required for them to use these structures fluently in their own writing. Complex, unusual patterns that students are unlikely to need at this stage in writing English have been avoided.

How to Use this Book

(a) *General*

Each of the first 28 lessons in the book contains a text giving examples of structures and patterns, exercises in comprehension, pattern practice, additional exercises on other items occurring in the text, and composition. These exercises are designed to teach what is presented in the lesson and for remedial work on what is already known, rather than to test students' knowledge. There is a short progress test at the end of each lesson aimed at ensuring that the main points contained in it have been thoroughly grasped.

The last seven lessons deal with the different kinds of composition students may be asked to write in examinations and emphasise structures especially appropriate to them.

In any course of this kind, where the intention is partly remedial, it may occasionally be necessary for teachers to revise structures that appear at a later stage in the book in order to correct persistent mistakes. The index should therefore be used for reference throughout the course.

(b) *Texts*

The texts cover the complete range of the types of composition students may be asked to write. Vocabulary likely to be new to students is not introduced for its own sake but only where the context justifies it, since experience demonstrates that context- ualisation is essential in learning new words. The vocabulary load is therefore comparatively light.

The main patterns exemplified in the text are picked out in italic type for easy reference. Students should not, however, assume from this that the rest of the text does not matter! Ignoring it would mean that the advantage of contextualisation for structures as well as vocabulary would be lost.

(c) *Comprehension*
These exercises are designed to prepare students for the multiple-choice questions now commonly used in examinations. The intention is not to catch students out but to ensure that they read the text carefully.

(d) *Words*
The words chosen are generally those that cause confusion. The object of these multiple-choice exercises is to encourage students to read words in the context of the passage, where the meaning will normally be perfectly clear, rather than to rely on word-for-word translation. There is also an opportunity for the teacher to explain why the alternative answers are wrong in all cases or wrong in the context.

(e) *Patterns*
The patterns should be practised after the text has been read. It is useful, especially if a particular pattern causes difficulty, for students to be asked to write one or two sentences of their own imitating it and for these to be used for further practice in class.

(f) *Other Grammatical Exercises*
Again, these should be done after the text has been read.

(g) *Composition*
The composition exercises in the first 28 lessons are aimed at encouraging students to use the structures and patterns they have just been practising for themselves. To this extent, the compositions are semi-guided. A short composition of about 100

words or so successfully reproducing the patterns is far more useful in the early stages of a course than over-ambitious attempts full of errors. By the time students reach the Composition Section of the book, they should be capable of working on their own, but models are nevertheless provided by means of the texts for the kinds of composition they will want to write.

(h) *Progress Tests*

These tests, together with the written composition exercises, should indicate whether what has been taught in the lesson has been thoroughly understood. It is often useful for a test of this nature to be attempted chorally in class once students have been given the opportunity to read through it so that they understand the context. Hesitation on the part of a number of students over a particular item will indicate immediately where further remedial work may be required.

(i) *Teacher's Guide*

A *Teacher's Guide* is available, containing practical advice, detailed notes on structures and answers to multiple-choice questions and progress tests.

Section One

Essential Structures and Patterns

1 Sunday Morning

It is Sunday morning. Rosemary is laying the table in
the dining room. The telephone rings.

ROSEMARY 212 8302.

WALTER Hello. Is that Rosemary? This is Walter
5 Jackson.

ROSEMARY Hello, Walter. How are you? Do you want to
speak to Roger?

WALTER Yes, please.

ROSEMARY Roger! He's just coming, Walter. How are
10 you _getting on_ in your new job?

WALTER I'm _enjoying it_. We live _quite near my office_
and of course we're not far from the New Forest.
I often take the family there at weekends.
There's not much to do here on Sundays, _except_
15 _go out in_ the car.

ROSEMARY _Roger's cleaning the car_ at the moment. It's a new
one and he's so proud of it that _he cleans it every_
Sunday. We never have time to go out in it
because he's always washing it, polishing it, or
20 getting underneath it to fix something. Here
he is at last. Give my regards to Carol, Walter.
We look forward to seeing you again one of
these days. 'Bye. _(recuerdos)_

ROGER Hello, Walter. What can I do for you?

25 WALTER I'm ringing about my next-door neighbour,
Bob Walker. He works as an engineer at a
factory near here but he wants to change
his job. I know him very well _so I_ can recommend him to you. Do you still intend to open a
30 branch office in Southampton?

ROGER Well, _you know these things always take time_ but
we expect everything to be ready soon. You
know Jim Crawford, our personnel manager,
don't you? I'll tell him about your friend and
35 he may be able to find something.

WALTER Fine. Yes, I remember Jim very well. Do you

and Rosemary still play bridge with him and his wife?

ROGER   Yes. In fact, we're waiting for them to arrive
40   for lunch. We expect them to be here in a few minutes. They come once a month and I think Jim looks forward to it. Judy goes out to work so I suppose *she often feels tired when she comes home.* I don't think Jim expects her to cook every
45   evening. He must live on sandwiches most of the time but Judy doesn't seem very grateful. *She's always telling him that he's too fat.*

WALTER   Poor fellow! I understand how he feels. I'm glad Carol doesn't go out to work, like Judy.
50 ROGER   Well, I hope Jim can do something for your friend. I expect I'll see you more often in future when we have our branch office near you.

WALTER   Good. I look forward to it. All the best for now and thanks for your help. Cheerio.
55 ROGER   Goodbye, Walter.

A   Comprehension

Which of the following statements is correct in the context of the passage?

(1) Walter (a) is looking for a job (b) wants to change his job (c) likes his new job.

(2) Rosemary and Roger never go out in their new car because (a) Roger has too much work to do at weekends (b) he is so proud of it that he does not want it to get dirty (c) he spends so much time taking care of it.

(3) (a) Roger is trying to open an office in Southampton (b) Roger's office is going to be moved to Southampton (c) Roger is planning to open an office in Southampton.

(4) Jim looks forward to visiting Roger and Rosemary because (a) he is getting fat (b) he seldom eats cooked meals (c) he only has a cooked meal once a month.

(5) (a) Walter is fat, like Jim (b) Walter feels sorry for

Jim because he is fat (c) Walter feels sorry for Jim because he has to eat a lot of sandwiches.

B Words

Choose the word or phrase from the alternatives given which is closest in meaning to the words in italics in the context of the passage.

(1) *Far* (1.12) (a) a long way (b) distant (c) away
(2) *Regards* (1.21) (a) looks (b) memories (c) good wishes
(3) *Intend* (1.29) (a) try (b) mean (c) attempt
(4) *He must live on sandwiches* (1.45) (a) I suppose he lives on sandwiches (b) he has to live on sandwiches (c) the doctor has told him to eat sandwiches
(5) *Grateful* (1.46) (a) agreeable (b) pleasant (c) thankful

C Patterns

Study the pattern in italic type in each case and then reproduce it, substituting the words given but taking care to form the verbs correctly, and change or put in articles, possessives, prepositions where necessary. The basic structure and word order will remain the same.

(1) *Roger's cleaning the car. He cleans it every Sunday*
    (a) Rosemary/lay/table/lay/lunchtime
    (b) The announcer/read/news/read/night
    (c) Walter/catch/bus/catch/morning
    (d) Rosemary/cook/dinner/cook/evening
    (e) Jim/paint/house/paint/year

(2) *She often feels tired when she comes home* ~~whenever , every time~~
    (a) He/usually/look/happy/receive/letter
    (b) They/always/appear/interested/ask/questions
    (c) She/frequently/take/taxi/be/in a hurry
    (d) Roger/never/use/car/go/work
    (e) They/seldom/eat/much/come/lunch

(3) *You know these things always take time*
    (a) I/believe/Jim/often/feel hungry
    (b) She/feel/Jim/occasionally/deserve a good meal
    (c) I/expect/Judy/sometimes/get tired

    (d) I/suppose/Roger/seldom/use/car
    (e) She/think/the programme/usually/begin at 11 o'clock

(4) *She is always telling him he is too fat*
    (a) I/catch/colds
    (b) He/wash and polish/car
    (c) They/make/trouble
    (d) She/complain about/weather
    (e) They/plan/changes/office.

D Word Order

Study the pattern in each case and reproduce it, as in Exercise C.

(1) *I know him very well*
    (a) I/love/her/much
    (b) He/speak/English/badly
    (c) He/play/bridge/well

(2) *Rosemary is laying the table in the dining room*
    (a) Roger/clean/car/garage
    (b) The children/play/games/park
    (c) He/write/letters/office

(3) *I often take the family (there) at weekends*
    (a) Judy/occasionally/cook/meal/in the evening
    (b) Roger/frequently/clean/car/on Sundays
    (c) We/always/have/holiday/at Christmas

(4) *Do you still intend to open an office in Southampton?*
    (a) she/want/buy/house/the country?
    (b) they/plan/have/picnic/the New Forest?
    (c) he/mean/spend/holidays/Italy?

E Expect, Hope, Look forward to, Wait (for)

Complete the sentences, using one of these verbs in the correct form.

(1) We .... them to be here in a few minutes.
(2) We .... seeing you again one of these days.
(3) I'm sorry you are ill. I .... you'll feel better soon.

(4) .... here, please. Mr. Jones will see you in a few minutes.
(5) I had to .... the bus for half an hour.
(6) I .... it won't rain tomorrow. We want to go out.
(7) We haven't heard from you for a long time. We .... you are well.
(8) We enjoyed the party very much and .... meeting you again.
(9) He is very late. I .... he missed his train.
(10) She often feels tired when she comes home so Jim seldom .... her to cook in the evening.

F Prepositions of Time

Complete the sentences with the correct preposition – *at, in, on*.

(1) There's not much to do here .... Sundays.
(2) It is usually quiet here .... Sunday mornings.
(3) He gets up early .... the morning and goes to bed late .... night.
(4) I often take the family to the New Forest .... weekends.
(5) The park looks beautiful .... autumn.
(6) It often snows .... January.
(7) I take my annual holiday .... the summer but I have a few days off .... Christmas and Easter.
(8) We expect them to arrive .... 12.30.
(9) I hope to meet them .... lunchtime.
(10) Lunch will be ready .... a few minutes.
(11) I look forward to seeing you at the party .*on*. Christmas Day.
(12) He was born .... 1 June 1936. *on the first of June 1936 / on June the fiftf 1936*
(13) He died .... 1852.
(14) The house was built .... the eighteenth century.
(15) I expect I'll see you more often .... future.

G Composition

Briefly explain what you usually do on Sundays.

✓ *PROGRESS TEST*
Choose the correct form in each case.

Judy $\frac{\text{is going}}{\text{goes}}$ to work every day, but she $\frac{\text{isn't working}}{\text{doesn't work}}$ today because it is Sunday. She $\frac{\text{is cooking}}{\text{cooks}}$ the dinner and $\frac{\text{his}}{\text{her}}$ husband $\frac{\text{is cleaning}}{\text{cleans}}$ the car. She $\frac{\text{isn't usually cooking}}{\text{doesn't usually cook}}$ a meal when she $\frac{\text{is coming}}{\text{comes}}$ home from work because she $\frac{\text{is feeling}}{\text{feels}}$ too tired but she $\frac{\text{is enjoying}}{\text{enjoys}}$ cooking and now she $\frac{\text{is making}}{\text{makes}}$ a special dish that Jim $\frac{\text{is liking.}}{\text{likes}}$ Jim $\frac{\text{is always complaining}}{\text{is complaining}}$ about having to eat sandwiches and she $\frac{\text{is knowing}}{\text{knows}}$ he $\frac{\text{is liking}}{\text{likes}}$ a change.

2 Guess Who's Coming to Dinner

BETTY Hello, Jane. How lucky to run into you. Can you
and Tom come to dinner tomorrow evening?

JANE I think so. I don't think we're going out.

BETTY I know it's rather short notice for you but *we've*
5   *just had a telegram from London.* Bob's cousin,
Lawrence, has just come back from South America.
He's coming for the weekend and he's going to
bring his wife. *They'll be staying with us here for the*
time being until they find somewhere to live. They've
10 →   only just got married so naturally we're looking
forward to meeting Carmen and we'd like to
introduce them both to all our friends.

JANE That sounds exciting. But I've just remembered
something. We're going to take the children to the
15   zoo tomorrow. I'm sure they won't be satisfied
unless we look at every animal and bird in the

place. It's going to be difficult for us <u>to get back
in time</u> for dinner.

BETTY   Well, we're not going to have dinner until quite
20   late, probably about eight o'clock. Lawrence and
his wife are coming tomorrow afternoon and that
will give them rather more time to get unpacked.

JANE   *I'm sure we'll be back <u>by eight</u>.* Who else is coming?

BETTY   I've just rung Alison, but she wasn't in. It's often
25   rather difficult for her <u>to get</u> a baby-sitter. By the
way, *what are you going to do about the children tomorrow
night?*

JANE   They'll be all right. Catherine, the girl next door,
will be quite pleased to look after them if I ask her.

30   BETTY   I hope you'll like the meal. I'm going to make a
special rice dish with chili sauce. I've made it before
from time to time but Carmen will probably
know much more about it <u>than I do</u>. Still, I want
them to feel at home.

35   JANE   What time shall we come, then?

BETTY   *The others are coming to the house about seven.* Then we'll
have time for a drink before dinner and everyone
can get to know each other.

JANE   We'll be looking forward to it. <u>I expect we'll be on</u>
40   →   <u>time. We'll be round about seven if we can manage</u>
come round?   it. I hope so, anyway.

BETTY   See you tomorrow, then. Goodbye for now.

A   Comprehension

Which of the following statements is correct in the context
of the passage?

(1) Bob is <u>(a)</u> Betty's cousin (b) Betty's husband <u>(c)</u>
Jane's husband.

(2) Betty and her husband are looking forward to
meeting Carmen because <u>(a)</u> she has just got married
(b) they are wondering what Lawrence's wife is like
<u>(c)</u> she is South American.

(3) Betty is going to have dinner at eight o'clock because
<u>(a)</u> Jane and her family will not be back before then
<u>(b)</u> people eat later in South America and she wants
to make her guests feel at home <u>(c)</u> she wants to give

Lawrence and Carmen an opportunity to get ready before they meet people.

(4) Alison (a) may not come to the dinner party because it is hard for her to find a baby-sitter (b) can't come to the dinner party because she can't find a baby-sitter (c) won't come to the party because she is out and won't be back in time.

(5) Jane and her husband will probably meet Lawrence and Carmen (a) at eight o'clock (b) before dinner (c) after dinner.

B Words

Choose the word or phrase from the alternatives given which is closest in meaning to the words in italics in the context of the passage.

(1) *It's rather short notice for you* (1.4) (a) I haven't given you much time to remark (b) I haven't given you much time to make arrangements (c) I haven't given you much advice

(2) *Exciting* (1.13) (a) emotional (b) excitable (c) very interesting

(3) *Unless we look* (1.16) (a) except we look (b) if we don't look (c) if we look

(4) *By eight* (1.23) (a) at eight (b) for eight (c) not later than eight

(5) *Who else is coming?* (1.23) (a) Which other person is coming? (b) Which other people is coming? (c) Which other people are coming?

(6) *She wasn't in* (1.24) (a) she was off (b) she was out (c) she was away

(7) *Look after* (1.29) (a) take care of (b) be careful with (c) take notice of

(8) *From time to time* (1.32) (a) regularly (b) occasionally (c) seldom

C Patterns

Study the pattern in italic type in each case and then reproduce it, substituting the words given but taking care to form the verbs correctly. Change or put in articles, possessives, prepositions where necessary.

(1) *We've just had a telegram from London*
   (a) I've/write/letter/cousin
   (b) He's/sell/radio/next-door neighbour
   (c) We've/send/present/bride
   (d) She's/receive/message/hospital
   (e) He's/tell/story/children

(2) *I'm sure we'll be back by eight*
   (a) glad/they'll/home/seven
   (b) hopeful/it'll/ready/tomorrow
   (c) pleased/it'll/over/midnight
   (d) certain/he'll/up/ten
   (e) confident/it'll/finished/next week.

(3) *What are you going to do about the children tomorrow?*
   (a) Where/spend/holidays/next summer?
   (b) Why/give up/job/next month?
   (c) Who/invite/party/Saturday?
   (d) Who/meet/cinema/tomorrow?
   (e) What time/have/dinner/tonight?

(4) *The others are coming to the house about seven*
   (a) The children/go/zoo/tomorrow
   (b) Betty/come/lunch/Sunday
   (c) Jane/go/Italy/next summer
   (d) Lawrence/fly/Rio de Janeiro/next week
   (e) We/have/party/Saturday

(5) *They'll be staying with us here for the time being*
   (a) I'll/watch/television/home/this evening
   (b) I'll/wait/you/church/tomorrow morning
   (c) We'll/look forward to/party/house/Saturday
   (d) They'll/travel/train/London/at this time tomorrow
   (e) He'll/write/letters/room/after dinner.

D   Quite and Rather

The girl next door will be quite pleased to look after the children
It's often rather difficult for her to get a baby-sitter
That will give them rather more time to get unpacked

Complete the following sentences, writing *quite* when you think the meaning is comparatively (good), *rather* when it suggests comparatively (bad), *rather* in all cases where a comparative adjective or adverb – e.g., *more, better* – is used.

(1) John found the examination .... easy but I thought it was .... difficult.
(2) I'm afraid we'll arrive .... late for the party.
(3) We're going to have dinner .... late because it will be more convenient.
(4) Jane thinks her cousin is .... intelligent but I've always found her .... boring.
(5) How are you? I'm .... well, thank you.
(6) She wasn't well yesterday but today she looks .... better.
(7) She's .... attractive but .... tall to be an actress.
(8) I feel .... tired. That case weighed .... more than I expected.

E Think So

Can you and Tom come to dinner tomorrow night?
I think so.
Use this construction and the verb in brackets to answer the following questions in the affirmative.

(1) Do you think you'll arrive in time for dinner? (hope)
(2) Are you going to have dinner late? (expect)
(3) Are they going to the zoo tomorrow? (believe)
(4) Is it going to be difficult for you to get back in time? (be afraid)
(5) Is Carmen South American? (suppose)

F Time (Collocations)

Complete the sentences with the correct preposition – *for, from, in, on, to*

(1) They'll be staying with us here .... the time being.
(2) It's going to be difficult to get back .... time for the party.
(3) The trains from this station never leave .... time.
(4) An inspector gets on the bus .... time .... time.

$\longrightarrow$ (5) Don't worry about it, sir. We'll repair it for you ..
no time.

G Particles

Complete the sentence with the correct particle – *back, in, out, over, round, up*

(1) I've just rung Alison but she didn't answer.
She must be . . . .
(2) I'm not sure if we'll be . . . . from the zoo by 6 o'clock.
(3) Excuse me. Is your husband . . . . ? I want to ask him some questions.
(4) If the dinner doesn't start until eight, it won't be . . . . till after midnight.
(5) We'll be . . . . as soon as we return from the zoo.
(6) He likes lying in bed. He wasn't . . . . when I rang him at 10 o'clock.

H Composition

You are going to have a party next Saturday because your brother has just come back from another country. Ring up a friend, inviting him/her to the party. Write the dialogue.

PROGRESS TEST

Choose the correct (or more common) form in each case.

Lawrence and Carmen $\dfrac{\text{were just arriving}}{\text{have just arrived}}$ at London

Airport. The plane arrived $\dfrac{\text{on}}{\text{in}}$ time but Carmen is $\dfrac{\text{quite}}{\text{rather}}$

tired after the long $\dfrac{\text{travel}}{\text{journey}}$ so they $\dfrac{\text{are going}}{\text{will go}}$ straight to a

hotel. Then Lawrence $\dfrac{\text{is going to}}{\text{will}}$ send a telegram to

Betty. $\dfrac{\text{Unless}}{\text{Except}}$ it is inconvenient, they $\dfrac{\text{will be staying}}{\text{are staying}}$ with

her and Bob $\dfrac{\text{during}}{\text{for}}$ the time being. They $\dfrac{\text{are going}}{\text{will go}}$ to

Betty's house tomorrow and Betty $\dfrac{\text{will have}}{\text{is going}}$ to have a

party in their honour.

3 The First Men on Venus *Vi:nəs*

If the population of the Earth goes on increasing at its
present rate, there will eventually not be enough resources
left to sustain life on the planet. *By the middle of the 21st
century,* if present trends continue, *we will have used up all the*
5   *oil* that drives our cars, for example. Even if scientists
develop new ways of feeding the human race, the crowded
conditions on Earth will make it necessary for us to look
for open space somewhere else. But none of the other
planets in our solar system are capable of supporting life at
10   present. One possible solution to the problem, however,
has recently been suggested by an American scientist,
Professor Carl Sagan.

Sagan believes that before the Earth's resources are
completely exhausted it will be possible to change the
15   atmosphere of Venus and so create a new world almost as
large as Earth itself. The difficulty is that Venus is much
hotter than the Earth and there is only a tiny amount of
water there.
Sagan proposes that algae, organisms that can live in
20   extremely hot or cold atmospheres and at the same time
produce oxygen, should be bred in conditions similar to
those on Venus. As soon as this has been done, the algae
will be placed in small rockets. Spaceships will then fly to
Venus and fire the rockets into the atmosphere. In a fairly
25   short time, the algae will break down the carbon dioxide
into oxygen and carbon.

*When the algae have done their work, the atmosphere will
become cooler* but before man can set foot on Venus, it will
be necessary for the oxygen to produce rain. The surface
30   of the planet will still be too hot for men to land on it but
the rain will eventually fall and in a few years something
like Earth will be reproduced on Venus.

If the experiments are successful, life will become possible there but it will not be pleasant at first. *When they go to
35   Venus, the first colonists will have to take plenty of water* with
them and get used to days and nights lasting 60 Earth-days.
But there will also be some advantages. The colonists will

/presión, tensión / .
atmosférica

live longer because their hearts will suffer less strain than
on Earth. Apart from that, *they will be exploring a new world*
40 *while those still on Earth are living in closed, uncomfortable*
conditions. Perhaps it will be the only way to ensure the
survival of the human race.
'hju:mən reis

A Comprehension

Choose which one of the following statements is correct
in the context of the passage.

(1) It will eventually become necessary for us to try to
colonise another planet because (a) the Earth will
have too many people on it (b) we will have used all
the oil that drives our cars (c) there are not enough
resources to sustain life on Earth.

(2) It is not possible for us to colonise Venus immediately
because (a) there is no water there (b) it is too far
away for us to go there (c) it is too hot to support
human life.

(3) Algae, are important for the colonisation of Venus
because (a) they can be bred in any conditions (b)
they produce oxygen (c) they can easily be carried
in spaceships.

(4) The first colonists on Venus will find life difficult
there because (a) they will suffer from heart strain
(b) there will be no water there (c) the days and
nights will be very long.

(5) One of the main advantages for the colonists will be
that (a) they will be the only survivors of the human
race (b) they will have comfortable houses (c) they
will have much more space than before.

B Words

Choose the word or phrase from the alternatives given
which is closest in meaning to the words in italics in the
context of the passage.

(1) *Goes on* (1.1) (a) follows (b) continues (c) starts
(2) *Supporting* (1.9) (a) maintaining (b) standing (c)
holding up

(3) *At present* (1.9) (a) presently (b) soon (c) now
(4) *Exhausted* (1.14) (a) tired (b) worn out (c) used up
(5) *Amount* (1.17) (a) number (b) quantity (c) pool
(6) *Break down* (1.25) (a) destroy (b) separate (c) collapse
(7) *Eventually* (1.31) (a) naturally (b) finally (c) inevitably
(8) *Like* (1.32) (a) as (b) similar to (c) attracted to
(9) *Plenty* (1.35) (a) some (b) a lot of (c) much
(10) *Apart from* (1.39) (a) besides (b) except (c) beside

C Patterns

Study the pattern in italic type in each case and then reproduce it, substituting the words given but taking care to form the verbs correctly. Change or put in articles, possessives, prepositions where necessary.

(1) *When they go to Venus, the first colonists will have to take* (plenty of) *water*
 (a) they/fly/Venus/they/fire/rockets
 (b) I/get/office/I/telephone/wife
 (c) you/go/library/you/take back/books
 (d) he/give up/job/they/look for/new manager
 (e) you/pay/bill/you/get/receipt

(2) *When the algae have done their work, the atmosphere will become cooler*
 (a) we/colonise/Venus/we/possess/new world
 (b) we/use up/the Earth's resources/we/colonise/other planets
 (c) you/finish/composition/teacher/collect/it
 (d) she/take/examinations/she/have/holiday
 (e) he/complete/experiments/he/check/results

(3) *They will be exploring a new world while those still on Earth are living in closed, uncomfortable conditions*
 (a) I/cook/dinner/he/read/paper
 (b) They/live/Rome/they/make/film
 (c) We/lie/sun/he/work/office
 (d) They/play/cards/I/watch/television
 (e) I/write/report/my secretary/have/lunch

(4) *By the middle of the 21st century, we will have used up all the oil*
 (a) the end/month/we spend/money

    (b) the end/evening/they/drink/wine
    (c) the end/year/they/complete/experiments
    (d) the beginning/next week/I/correct/papers
    (e) the end/day/he/install/machines

D Too and Enough

(1) *He is too shy to be a good salesman*
He is not self-confident enough to be a good salesman

Study these examples and rewrite the sentences, using *not*
+ the opposite adjective + *enough* instead of *too* +
adjective.

    (a) He is too ill to make the journey.
    (b) She is too plain to become an actress.
    (c) I am too short to reach the shelf.
    (d) She is too fat to wear a bikini.
    (e) They are too young to go out alone.
    (f) She is too careless to look after children.
    (g) They are too lazy to pass the examination.
    (h) The train is too slow to get us there in time.

(2) *The surface of the planet will be too hot for men to land on it*
The surface of the planet will not be cool enough for men to
land on it

Change the sentences in the same way as in (D) (1)

    (a) The Earth's resources will be too small for the
        population to survive.
    (b) The atmosphere is too hot for us to live there.
    (c) The street is too narrow for cars to pass one
        another.
    (d) The conditions are too bad for them to climb the
        mountain.
    (e) The sky is too cloudy for them to launch the
        spaceship.
    (f) The court is too wet for us to play tennis.
    (g) That bed will be too uncomfortable for her to
        sleep in.
    (h) The river is too dirty for us to bathe in.

E As and Like (1)

(1) *Carol doesn't go out to work, like Judy (her).*
Carol doesn't go out to work, as Judy (she) does.

Study these two sentences and complete the sentences below, using *as* and *like* in each case.
  (a) He travels to London by train every day,.... (I)
  (b) I work in an office, ... (my father)
  (c) I believe in freedom, ... (you)
  (d) He writes novels, ... (she)
  (e) He lives over the road, ... (Mrs. Croft)

(2) *He works as an engineer* (profession)
   He climbs trees like a monkey (comparison)

Complete the following sentences, using *as* when the sentence indicates a person's status or profession, *like* when a comparison is being made.
  (a) I like working .... a teacher.
  (b) She looks .... her father.
  (c) My uncle is always borrowing money but he lives .... a king.
  (d) He gave up his job .... a journalist and started writing novels.
  (e) He is over forty years old but he runs about .... a boy of fifteen.

(3) *As always, there are very few people about on Sunday morning*

Repeat the pattern, using the words supplied.
  (a) usual/a lot of/at the football match
  (b) you know/a number of/in the same office
  (c) you can see/not many/in the audience

(4) *Something like Earth will be reproduced on Venus*

Repeat the pattern, using the words supplied.
  (a) Someone/you/chosen for the job
  (b) Scientists/him/needed in the future
  (c) Experiments/that/made on other planets

F Composition

  (1) Briefly describe the changes that you think will have taken place on Earth by the end of the century if the population goes on increasing at its present rate.
  (2) Say what you think life on Venus will be like when the first colonists arrive there (assuming Professor Sagan's plan has been successful).

√ *PROGRESS TEST*

Choose the correct form in each case.

Before they $\frac{\text{will fly}}{\text{fly}}$ to Venus the first men chosen to live

there $\frac{\text{will have to}}{\text{are having to}}$ get used to the conditions there. While

the algae $\frac{\text{are doing}}{\text{will do}}$ their work of producing oxygen, the

first colonists $\frac{\text{are learning}}{\text{will be learning}}$ how to survive in the new

world. When they $\frac{\text{go}}{\text{are going}}$ to Venus, they $\frac{\text{will take}}{\text{have taken}}$

plenty of water. By that time, it $\frac{\text{has rained}}{\text{will have rained}}$ $\frac{\text{for}}{\text{during}}$ a

long time and the temperature of the planet $\frac{\text{will have fallen.}}{\text{will fall.}}$

But at first the water on Venus $\frac{\text{will be too}}{\text{is} \quad \text{enough}}$ dangerous

for men to risk drinking it. When the scientists $\frac{\text{will test}}{\text{have tested}}$

it, they $\frac{\text{will decide}}{\text{are deciding}}$ if it $\frac{\text{will be}}{\text{is}} \frac{\text{pure enough}}{\text{enough pure}}$ for people

to drink it.

4 Moving Experiences

27 Oak Tree Avenue,
Southbury,
Essex.

not installmen

8 July 1972

Dear Mary,

As you can see, we have just moved into our new house. In fact, *we took up residence three days ago.* We received your letter last week at our old address in High Street but I

(*move in*)

5   haven't had time to answer it until now.

Have you ever moved house? As you can imagine, George and I have been working hard putting the house in order and *the children have been having a wonderful time for the past three days*, playing hide-and-seek all over the house and

10 getting under the furniture and behind the packing cases. Although *we haven't had a moment's rest since we moved in*, it has been an exciting time for us all. We have always wanted to live here on the outskirts of the town, only a stone's throw from open country, and when we saw that

15 this house was for sale, we jumped at the chance and put down a deposit on it straightaway.

George has finished decorating all the rooms except the kitchen. For some reason that he didn't explain to me, he put off painting it until last so we have had to live out

20 of tins because I haven't been able to cook proper meals. However, experience has taught me not to argue with him about such matters.

Several years ago, soon after we were married, George put up a ladder against the outside of the house. I was

25 supposed to hold it steady while he painted the window frames upstairs, but I heard the telephone ringing and let go of the ladder. George slid to the ground. The wet paint brush went up his nose and the tin of paint fell on his head. *He has never forgotten the incident* or let me forget it.

30 He must have finished painting the kitchen by now. I wonder if he has been experimenting with something new. Regards from us all. Our best wishes to David. We look forward to hearing from you.

Affectionately,
35 Anne

P.S. I have just come back from the kitchen. When I went in, I had the shock of my life. I thought George was covered in blood. He has painted the walls bright red but spilled half the paint over himself. Still, I have learnt

40 to put up with George so I suppose I'll learn to put up with his idea of a kitchen.

A Comprehension

Choose which one of the following statements is correct in the context of the passage.

(1) Mary knows that Anne has moved into a new house because (a) she has been there (b) the new address appears at the top of the letter (c) she wrote to Anne at the new address.

(2) George and Anne (a) preferred living in the centre of town (b) wanted to move to the country (c) have always wanted to live away from the centre of town.

(3) Anne hasn't been able to cook proper meals because (a) she hasn't unpacked the cooker (b) George is only now decorating the kitchen (c) the children have got in her way.

recieu (ahora)

(4) Anne and George (a) have just got married (b) have been married for three years (c) have been married for a number of years.

(5) Anne (a) thinks that George has almost certainly finished painting the kitchen (b) thinks George had to finish painting the kitchen that day (c) had told George that he must finish painting the kitchen that day.

B   Words

Choose the word or phrase from the alternatives given which is closest in meaning to the words in italics in the context of the passage.

(1) *Hard* (1.7) (a) hardly (b) much (c) a great deal

(2) *On the outskirts* (1.13) (a) in the country (b) outside the town (c) on the edge of the town

(3) *Open country* (1.14) (a) land with few houses (b) land with few hills or mountains (c) uncultivated land

(4) *Chance* (1.15) (a) opportunity (b) luck (c) occasion

(5) *Straightaway* (1.16) (a) direct (b) immediately (c) without thinking

(6) *Live out of tins* (1.19) (a) have all our possessions in tins (b) eat tinned food (c) eat meals cooked in tins

(7) *Put up* (1.24) (a) built (b) established (c) leant

(8) *Experimenting with* (1.31) (a) experiencing (b) trying out (c) trying on

(9) *Shock* (1.37) (a) crash (b) blow (c) greatest surprise

(10) *Spilled* (1.39) (a) fell (b) dropped (c) let fall

C Patterns

Study the pattern in italic type in each case and then reproduce it, substituting the words given but taking care to form the verbs correctly. Change or put in articles, possessives, prepositions where necessary.

(1) *Have you ever moved house?*
   (a) read/'Hamlet'?
   (b) play/hide-and-seek?
   (c) live/the country?
   (d) visit/zoo?
   (e) work/factory?

(2) *He has never forgotten the incident*
   (a) They/decorate/house
   (b) We/meet/Queen
   (c) I/write/novel
   (d) She/drive/car
   (e) He/tell/lie

(3) *The children have been having a wonderful time for the past three days*
   (a) George/paint/kitchen/four hours
   (b) We/live/London/six months
   (c) She/study/French/year
   (d) I/work/estate agent's/two years
   (e) He/stay/his mother's/week

(4) *We haven't had a moment's rest since we moved in*
   (a) He/do/an honest day's work/be born
   (b) I/have/a good night's sleep/the motorway/be built
   (c) He/pay/a week's rent/he/move in
   (d) You/make/a single mistake/class/begin
   (e) They/lose/a single game/championship/start

(5) *We took up residence three days ago*
   (a) She/pack cases/two days
   (b) We/receive letter/a week
   (c) I/ring the estate agent's/an hour
   (d) He/sell house/a year
   (e) They/go abroad/a fortnight

D   For, Since and Ago

(1) *The children have been having a wonderful time for three days*
The children have been having a wonderful time since we
moved in/since Tuesday
We moved in three days ago/on Tuesday

Study these sentences and complete the sentences below using *for, since, ago* and a past time expression.

(a) George has been working in the kitchen for . . . *3 days*
George has been working in the kitchen since. . *Tuesday*
George started working in the kitchen *3 days* . . . . ago
George started working in the kitchen at. *Tuesday*

G.& A are }
were } married (b) George and Anne have been married for . *7 years*
George and Anne have been married since . . . *1978*
George and Anne got married *7 years* . . . ago
George and Anne got married in . *1978*

(c) I have been learning English for . . *10 years*
I have been learning English since . . *1975*
I started learning English *10 years* . . . ago
I started learning English in . *1975*

(d) I have been living in this town for . *8 years*
I have been living in this town since . *1977*
I came to live in this town *8 years* . . . ago
I came to live in this town in *1977*

(2) *He worked in France for five years*
He worked in France from 1962 to 1967

For can be used in the past tense when the period referred to is finished.

Rewrite the following sentences, using *for*.

(a) He taught at the Institute from 1964 to 1968.
(b) Elizabeth I was Queen of England from 1558 to 1603.
(c) The Second World War lasted from 1939 to 1945.
(d) He was champion of the world from 1920 to 1927.

E   Phrasal Verbs – Put

Complete the sentences with one of the following prepositions – *down, off* (2), *on* (2), *out, up* (3), *up with*

B

(1) How much did you have to put ....*down* as a deposit on your house?

(2) It's cold. Put your coat .*on*. when you go out.

(3) George put .*up*. a ladder against the wall.

(4) He is very bad-tempered. I don't know how she can put .*up*. .*with*.him.

(5) It's dark in here. I'll put the light .*on*.

(6) We'll have to put the match .*off*. until next week because of the rain.

(7) I'll be all right. Please don't put yourself .*out*. on my account.

(8) 'Put .*up*. your hands'! shouted the bank robber.

(9) He talked so much while we were playing chess that he put me .*off*. my game.

(10) They arrived suddenly/with nowhere to stay so I put them .*up*. for the night. *without anywhere to stay*

handwritten margin notes:
on — light, coat
out — light, himself for s.o
off — the match, puts s.o. off s.th.
up — ladder, hands, s.o. for certain time

F Composition

(1) You have just moved into a new house. Describe what you have been doing in the two days since you arrived.

(2) You have been staying at a hotel by the seaside for the past three days. Describe what you have been doing in that time.

PROGRESS TEST

Choose the correct form of the verb in each case and choose the correct word (*for*, *since* or *ago*) in the context.

$\frac{For}{Since}$ the last three days, I $\frac{\text{have been working}}{\text{am working}}$ hard

decorating our new house. When we $\frac{\text{have moved}}{\text{moved}}$ in three

days $\frac{since,}{ago,}$ everything $\frac{\text{has been}}{\text{was}}$ in a mess (but) now I

$\frac{\text{have almost finished}}{\text{have almost been finishing}}$ the job. Today I $\frac{\text{have been}}{\text{am working}}$

$\frac{\text{working since}}{\text{for}}$ breakfast and $\frac{\text{am not having}}{\text{have not had}}$ anything to

eat. Anne $\frac{\text{has brought}}{\text{brought}}$ me a sandwich an hour $\frac{ago}{since}$

(but) I have told / told her not to come into the kitchen. I have never forgotten / am never forgetting what happened / has happened several years since / ago when she has tried / tried to help me. I am not having / have not had many accidents for / since then (but) Anne has often been / has often warned warning me to be careful. She has warned / warned me again this morning at breakfast-time (but) I have been working / am working since / for four hours and nothing goes / has gone wrong. Damn! Now I dropped / have dropped the tin of paint. Has anything like that ever been happening / happened to you?

5 Return to Farley

14 York Road,
Seaton,
Sussex.
22 May 1973

Dear Margaret,

Something that happened the other day reminded me that I haven't written to you for a long time. I suppose most brothers are as forgetful as I am.

5   The firm sent me to Farley. The representative who usually deals with clients in that area was away ill, so I had to stand in for him. *I am so used to travelling about the country in my job* that it's odd that I'd never been back to Farley since we were evacuated there during the war but,

10   as you know, I usually cover the South Coast.

I finished my business with our client in the morning and went to have lunch at the Ship Café for old times' sake. Do you remember having tea there with Mother and Father when they used to come down from London to see
→15 us? I stood around in Church Street for five minutes before I realised that a <u>building site</u> where some workmen were digging foundations was where the Ship used to be. I had to go to The Black Bull instead.

After lunch I walked round the town. Broadwood
20 Crescent is still standing but the house where we lived with Mrs. Lake is now in very bad condition and the garden is full of weeds. Mrs. Lake must have moved away long ago. She couldn't stand weeds. I needn't remind you of that. I remember that she used to make you pull them up.

25 The biggest shock came when I climbed Broadwood Hill. *The little school we used to go to has disappeared* and now there is a vast comprehensive school in its place. *The fields* at the top of the hill *where we picked blackberries are built on now.* There is a new <u>housing estate</u> that stretches
30 as far as the motorway and has taken in the villages in between. Do you remember those Sunday walks? They still stand out in my memory. Mrs Lake used to make us put on our best clothes and we walked to Barton or Compton. She never let us stop and look at the cows or
35 play hide-and-seek in the trees and hedges. We always had to be well-behaved. But *whenever she met an acquaintance* of hers *we would play games* while her back was turned. There are no hedges now, I'm afraid. Just rows and rows of houses.
40 I thought you would be interested to hear how Farley has changed. <u>Remember me</u> to Harry.
With love,
Jack

A   Comprehension

Which of the following statements is correct in the context of the passage?

(1) Jack had not been to Farley before because (a) he had unpleasant memories of the town (b) the

representative there had never been ill (c) he usually deals with clients on the South Coast.

(2) He stood around in Church Street for a few minutes because (a) he was interested in what the workmen were doing (b) he was wondering what had happened to the Ship Café (c) he was waiting for The Black Bull to open.

(3) Mrs Lake (a) no longer lives in the same house (b) no longer looks after her garden (c) stopped pulling the weeds up when Jack and Margaret left.

(4) The villages of Barton and Compton (a) were knocked down when the motorway was built (b) were knocked down and replaced by a comprehensive school (c) are now part of Farley.

(5) When they went out for a walk with Mrs. Lake on Sundays, Jack and Margaret (a) never used to play (b) only played when Mrs. Lake was not looking (c) sometimes met friends of theirs.

B Words

Choose the word or phrase from the alternatives given which is closest in meaning to the words in italics in the context of the passage.

(1) *The other day* (1.2) (a) the next day (b) a few days ago (c) yesterday

(2) *Deals with* (1.6) (a) treats (b) argues with (c) does business with

(3) *Stand in for him* (1.7) (a) take his place (b) stand up in his place (c) exchange jobs with him.

(4) *I am so used to travelling* (1.7) (a) I used to travel so much (b) I am so tired of travelling (c) I am so accustomed to travelling

(5) *Odd* (1.8) (a) strange (b) rare (c) uneven

(6) *For old times' sake* (1.12) (a) because it was a very old place (b) because I had a sentimental affection for it (c) because they make good tea there

(7) *As far as* (1.30) (a) until (b) beyond (c) up to

(8) *Would* (1.37) (a) should (b) (past form of) will (c) used to

(9) *I'm afraid* (1.38) (a) I'm shocked (b) I'm sorry to say (c) I feel nervous

(10) *Rows* (1.38) (a) files (b) lines (c) arguments

C Patterns

Study the pattern in italic type in each case and then reproduce it, substituting the words given but taking care to form the verbs correctly. Change or put in articles, possessives, prepositions where necessary.

(1) *The fields where we picked blackberries are built on now*
   (a) college/I/study languages/closed
   (b) theatre/Shakespeare/present plays/destroyed
   (c) café/we/have tea/demolished

(2) *The little school we used to go to has disappeared*
   (a) cinema/I/go to/been closed down
   (b) house/they/live in/been knocked down
   (c) restaurant/we/eat at/been shut down

(3) *Whenever she met an acquaintance we would play games*
   (a) Uncle Charles/visit/the children/he/tell stories
   (b) Mother/make/bread/we/ask for more
   (c) They/visit/Farley/they/go to the Ship Café

(4) *I am used to travelling about the country in my job*
   (a) He/work long hours/. . . .job
   (b) She/meet people/. . . .job
   (c) I/deal with clients/. . . .job

D Make and Let

Mrs Lake used to make us put on our best clothes
She never let us stop and look at the cows
Study these sentences and complete those below with suitable verbs.

(1) Mrs Lake used to make Margaret . . . the weeds up.
(2) She never lets the children . . . up late.
(3) He made us . . . the exercise again.
(4) The farmer let us . . . . football in his field.

(5) She makes the children *clean* .... their teeth before they go to school.
(6) The policeman made them *put* .... the car out of the way.
(7) A good teacher always lets the students .... *ask* questions.
(8) The agent let us .... *take* the keys of the house so that we could look it over.

E Remember and Remind

Complete the sentences, using one of these verbs in the correct tense.

(1) Something that happened the other day .... *reminded* me of my childhood.
(2) Do. you .... *remember* having tea at the Ship Café?
(3) I needn't .... *remind* you of Mrs Lake's garden.
(4) I .... *remember* you pulling up the weeds. (*I remember you pulled up the weeds*)
(5) Please .... *remember* to write to me soon.
(6) I can't .... *remember* where I put her letter.
(7) .... *Remind* me to get up early tomorrow morning.
(8) I know that I posted the letter. I .... *remember* putting it in the box.
(9) You .... *remind* me of someone I knew when I was young.
(10) .... *Remember* me to Harry.

F Phrasal Verbs – Stand

Complete the sentences with one of the following prepositions – *around, by (2), for (2), in for, out, over, up for, up to.*

(1) The usual representative was ill so I had to stand *in* . *for* . him.
(2) I stood *around* in Church Street for five minutes, looking for the Ship Café.
(3) The Sunday walks we took with Mrs Lake still stand *out* . in my memory.
(4) If you're not prepared to stand *up* . *for* . yourself, how can we help you?
(5) The letters U N O stand *for* .. the United Nations Organisation.

stand out = sobresalir

(handwritten margin notes: atenerse / by — quedarse sin hacer nada / for — representar — aguantar / up for = defend verbally / up to = resist)

(6) I can't bear my boss standing *over* me while I am working. (What verb could be used instead of 'bear'?)

(7) My leg is better but I don't think it would stand *up* *put up with* . *to*. a lot of exercise.

(8) I will stand *by*. the agreement.

(9) Do you expect me to stand *by*. . when I see a friend of mine being attacked?

(10) I won't stand . *for*. any more insults.

G Pronunciation (1)

In each group of four words below, three words rhyme but one does not. Choose the word that does not rhyme with the others in the group.

(1)	(a) rows	(b) knows	(c) goes	(d) cows
(2)	(a) were	(b) there	(c) care	(d) fair
(3)	(a) more	(b) far	(c) war	(d) law
(4)	(a) break	(b) make	(c) sake	(d) weak
(5)	(a) brother	(b) other	(c) bother	(d) mother
(6)	(a) full	(b) pull	(c) bull	(d) dull
(7)	(a) state	(b) eight	(c) height	(d) great
(8)	(a) coast	(b) post	(c) most	(d) lost
(9)	(a) lead (v)	(b) bread	(c) dead	(d) instead
(10)	(a) mind	(b) wind(n)	(c) kind	(d) find

H Composition

Describe the changes that have taken place in a town or village you know well in the last ten or twenty years.

PROGRESS TEST

Choose the correct alternative in each case.

I $\frac{\text{am used}}{\text{used}}$ to travelling so I don't always $\frac{\text{remind}}{\text{remember}}$ the

places I have visited but some stand $\frac{\text{up}}{\text{out}}$ in my memory.

Farley $\frac{\text{used to be}}{\text{was usually}}$ a small country town. The main street

ran $\frac{\text{as far as}}{\text{until}}$ the fields a mile $\frac{\text{away}}{\text{far}}$ from the town centre.

Now there is a vast housing estate on the fields where

I $\frac{\text{was seeing}}{\text{used to see}}$ cows.

Whenever I $\frac{\text{passed}}{\text{past}}$ them $\frac{\text{on}}{\text{in}}$ my way to Farley I $\frac{\text{would}}{\text{did}}$ stop. They $\frac{\text{reminded}}{\text{remembered}}$ me of my childhood. Cows always make me $\frac{\text{thinking}}{\text{think}}$ of the farm where I $\frac{\text{had lived}}{\text{used to live}}$ when I was a boy.

6 Fire, Fire

One evening last week my wife and I were sitting quietly at home. *She was looking at the television while I was reading a book.* Suddenly we heard a loud bang. I supposed that the old lady in the flat above ours was moving the furniture about. *My wife was afraid that the noise would wake the baby.* She turned down the television and a moment later we heard someone calling for help.

I ran upstairs. The old lady's door was shut but I could see smoke coming through the letter box and under the door and could smell something burning. 'The flat is on fire,' I shouted down to my wife. 'Ring the fire brigade.'

I banged on the door but the old lady took a long time to answer. I was turning over in my mind the idea of breaking the door down when she finally appeared.

'I was having a bath,' she said, 'when the water heater in the kitchen blew up.'

'Why didn't you open the door?' I asked her.

'I was getting dressed when you knocked,' she said, looking embarrassed.

I took her downstairs to our flat. Then *I ran back, went inside the old lady's flat and turned the gas off* to prevent another explosion. Smoke was pouring out of the kitchen and the heater was in flames. Just then I heard a fire engine arriving outside and the heavy footsteps of the firemen on

25   the stairs. I looked round and noticed two of them standing in the doorway. 'It's in here,' I said. 'You turned
up promptly, I must say.'

    When I got back to our flat my wife was making the old lady *a
cup of tea.* Soon afterwards, the fire chief came in to ask
30   some questions. It turned out that the fire was not very
serious and the firemen were already putting it out. When
they left my wife went up with the old lady to help her
clear up the mess.

    When she returned, my wife remarked: 'It's all right
35   now. Nothing was damaged except the heater. But wasn't
it lucky that Baby slept through all that noise?'

    She took the teacups into the kitchen and I heard her
scream and the cups crash to the floor. When I got there,
water was dripping slowly from the ceiling and forming a
40   pool on the floor. The baby woke up at last and started to cry.

A   Comprehension

Which of the following statements is correct in the context
of the passage?

(1) My wife was afraid because (a) she thought the flat
above was on fire (b) she heard the lady upstairs
calling for help (c) she thought the noise would wake
the baby.

(2) I knew the flat was on fire because (a) I heard the
lady calling for help (b) I saw smoke coming through
the letter-box (c) the fire brigade arrived.

(3) The old lady did not open the door because (a) she
was putting the fire out (b) she was getting dressed
(c) she did not hear me banging on the door.

(4) When I got back to my flat (a) the old lady was
talking to the fire chief (b) two firemen were standing
in the doorway (c) my wife was making the old lady
a cup of tea.

(5) My wife screamed because (a) she saw the water
dripping from the ceiling (b) the cups crashed to the
floor (c) the baby started to cry.

B   Words

Choose the word or phrase from the alternatives given

which is closest in meaning to the words in italics in the context of the passage.

(1) *Turned down* (1.6) (a) put out (b) reduced the sound of (c) switched off.
(2) *Later* (1.7) (a) more recently (b) nearer (c) afterwards.
(3) *Turning over* (1.13) (a) considering (b) making up (c) changing.
(4) *Blew up* (1.16) (a) began to burn (b) exploded (c) pushed air upwards
(5) *Embarrassed* (1.19) (a) confused (b) nervous (c) uncomfortable.
(6) *Noticed* (1.25) (a) remarked (b) paid attention to (c) saw.
(7) *Remarked* (1.34) (a) noticed (b) told (c) said.
(8) *Lucky* (1.36) (a) fortunate (b) occasional (c) a good chance.
(9) *Forming* (1.39) (a) establishing (b) making (c) shaping
(10) *At last* (1.40) (a) at least (b) finally (c) at the end.

C Patterns

Study the pattern in italic type in each case and then reproduce it, substituting the words given but taking care to form the verbs correctly. Change or put in articles, possessives, prepositions where necessary.

(1) *I ran back, went inside the old lady's flat and turned the gas off*
 (a) He/come in/close door/take coat off.
 (b) She/get up/go bathroom/turn tap on.
 (c) The firemen/drive up/run stairs/put fire out.
 (d) The secretary/sit down/open envelope/take letter out.
(2) *When I got back to our flat my wife was making a cup of tea*
 (a) I/knock/door/old lady/have/bath.
 (b) We/turn/television/announcer/read/news.
 (c) He/arrive/cinema/girl-friend/wait/him.
 (d) The secretary/go/room/boss/telephone/customer.
(3) *She was looking at the television while I was reading a book*
 (a) My wife/cook/dinner/I/write/letter.

(b) The children/play/hide-and-seek/George/paint/ kitchen.

(c) I/work/office/they/lie/beach.

(d) The hairdresser/cut/hair/she/read/magazine.

(4) *My wife was afraid that the noise would wake the baby*

(a) I/frightened/we/miss/train.

(b) My wife/terrified/I/drop/tray.

(c) We/confident/he/win/match.

(d) They/hopeful/he/marry/daughter.

D   Infinitive and Participle

Verbs like 'see' and 'hear' can be followed by an infinitive (without 'to') or by a present participle.

I heard her scream

We heard someone calling for help

Complete the sentences below with suitable verbs, using the infinitive when you think the action was short and complete, the present participle when it probably continued for some time.

(1) I saw water .... *dripping* from the ceiling.

(2) He saw the little girl .... *throwing* the toy out of the window.

(3) I heard her .... *saying* 'Hello'.

(4) He heard the birds .... in the garden.

(5) I saw smoke .... *coming* through the letter-box.

(6) I noticed two firemen .... *standing* in the doorway.

(7) I watched them .... *playing* football.

(8) He saw the thief .... *stealing* the girl's handbag and *running* away.

E   Phrasal Verbs – Turn

Complete the sentences with one of the following prepositions – *down* (2), *into*, *off*, *on*, *out* (2), *over*, *to*, *up*.

on → light
off → light
out (prove) intr.
(produce) tr.
down ← TV, job
up ← TV, (appear)
to → start

(1) My wife turned *down* the television because it was too loud.

(2) I was turning *over* — *consider* .... in my mind the idea of breaking the door down.

(3) I turned the gas *off*. to prevent an explosion.

(4) I was surprised that the firemen turned *up*. so promptly.

(5) It turned *out*. that the fire was not serious.

(6) He turned *down*. the job because they did not offer him enough money.

(7) Please turn the light *on* . . . . I can't see well enough to read.

(8) This factory turns .*out*. a thousand cars a day.

(9) At 0°C, water turns *into* ice.

(10) He could not earn enough money to live as a writer, so he turned .*to*.. teaching.

F Prepositions of Place

Complete the sentences with one of the following – *above, against, at, below, from, in, into, of, on, opposite, through, under.*

(1) We have just moved *into*. our new house.

(2) We moved *in*.. three days ago.

(3) He stood the ladder *against* the wall.

(4) My wife and I were sitting quietly .*at*. home.

(5) There was a fire in the flat *above* ours.

(6) I saw smoke coming *through* the letter-box and *under* the door.

(7) The heater .*in*. the kitchen was in flames.

(8) I met the firemen .*on*. the stairs.

(9) Water was dripping *from*. the ceiling and forming a pool .*on*. the floor.

(10) I live .*in*. Nelson Street. The block of flats where I live is the first .*on*. the left if you come *into* the street *from* Wellington Road. There is a pillar box .*at*. the corner. My flat is *on*. the third floor. An old lady lives *under/below* us and a young couple live .*opposite* us. Our best friends, Frank and Jennifer, live .*on*. the other side .*of*. the street .*in*. the house . . . . ours. *opposite*

G Composition

You heard a neighbour calling for help because (a) her flat was on fire (b) she had fallen down and broken her arm (c) she had come out without her key and could not get in. Briefly explain what you saw and did in one of these situations.

PROGRESS TEST

While I $\frac{\text{was having}}{\text{had}}$ a bath I suddenly heard something

$\frac{\text{explode \quad in}}{\text{exploding into}}$ the kitchen. When I got there, the heater

was $\frac{\text{on}}{\text{in}}$ flames and smoke $\frac{\text{poured}}{\text{was pouring}}$ out of the room.

I called for help and soon $\frac{\text{was hearing}}{\text{heard}}$ Mr Taylor

$\frac{\text{to come}}{\text{coming}}$ up the stairs. I couldn't open the door straight-

away because I $\frac{\text{got}}{\text{was getting}}$ dressed. When I $\frac{\text{was letting}}{\text{let}}$

him $\frac{\text{in,}}{\text{into,}}$ he turned the gas $\frac{\text{off.}}{\text{over.}}$ The firemen soon arrived

to put the fire $\frac{\text{outside.}}{\text{out.}}$ Mrs Taylor helped me clear up the

mess. 'It's a good thing they turned $\frac{\text{in}}{\text{up}}$ so quickly,' she

$\frac{\text{noticed,}}{\text{remarked,}}$ 'and they $\frac{\text{didn't make}}{\text{weren't making}}$ much noise. I was

afraid that they $\frac{\text{would wake}}{\text{waked}}$ the baby.'

7 The Road to Bordeaux

The French Grand Prix of 1903 is still remembered as one
of the most tragic motor races in history. It was not the
first Grand Prix. Motor races had begun soon after the
invention of the car and *there had already been several*
5 *national championships* of France *before this one*. But what
happened during the race ensured that it would be the
last run on public roads.

The best drivers in Europe arrived at Versailles for the
start. Over 300 competitors had entered for the race,

10   among them several whose names later became household
       words – Rolls (of Rolls-Royce), Marcel Renault, Lancia,
       Bugatti. There was even a lady-driver, Madame du Gast.
       As the King of Spain, Alfonso *XIII*, was a keen motorist,
       the organisers had agreed that on this occasion *the race would be*
15   *run from Paris to Madrid* but the Spanish crowds who were
       already preparing to welcome the drivers at the finish
       never saw them.

       The trouble was that *the* thousands of *people who lined the*
       route to watch the race *did not realise how powerful cars had*
20   *become in a few years*. The first winner of the Grand Prix
       had covered the distance from Paris to Rouen at an
       average speed of 10 miles per hour but now there were
       cars that were capable of going much faster. Apart from
       the crowds, the drivers had other problems. In those days,
25   the local government authorities did not usually have the
       roads surfaced with asphalt and so the cars raised clouds
       of dust as they went by, which made it almost impossible
       for the drivers behind to see.

       The race had hardly begun when a woman crossed the
30   road in front of a car and was knocked down. Soon
       afterwards, a driver swerved to avoid a child and crashed
       into the crowd, killing three people. Another drove into a
       wall, trying not to hit a dog, and *Madame du Gast, who had*
       been keeping up with the leaders, lost two hours while she took care
35   *of him* and his mechanic.

       By the time the surviving *drivers reached Bordeaux, the number*
       of accidents had risen even more and the newspapers had
       begun a campaign to have the race stopped. The Govern-
       ment gave way to the pressure of public opinion. Gabriel,
40   the driver who had arrived in Bordeaux first, was awarded
       the prize. In spite of the conditions, he had achieved an
       average speed of nearly 70 miles per hour. But in view of
       what had happened the authorities decided that in future
       motor races would have to be held on specially constructed
45   tracks where the public would be protected.

A   Comprehension

Which of the following statements is correct in the context
of the passage?

(1) The French Grand Prix of 1903 is still remembered because (a) it was the first motor race run on public roads (b) it was the first motor race (c) there were so many accidents during the race.

(2) The organisers had agreed that on this occasion the race would be run from Paris to Madrid because (a) Alfonso *XIII* was such a keen motorist (b) Alfonso *XIII* was taking part in it (c) the Spanish people wanted to see it.

(3) The race was dangerous to the public because (a) the drivers drove so fast (b) they did not realise that cars were so fast (c) there were so many cars on the road.

(4) Madame du Gast lost two hours in the race because (a) she knocked down a dog (b) she drove into a wall (c) she looked after another driver who had crashed.

(5) The government stopped the race in Bordeaux because (a) they felt sorry for people watching (b) the newspapers had criticised it (c) Alfonso *XIII* had said that it would be too dangerous to run the race in Spain.

B Words

Choose the word or phrase from the alternatives given which is closest in meaning to the words in italics in the context of the passage.

(1) *During the race* (1.6) (a) while the race was taking place (b) for the duration of the race (c) for the race

(2) *Entered for* (1.9) (a) taken part in (b) started (c) put their names down for

(3) *Household words* (1.10) (a) names of household products (b) names known everywhere (c) names of houses

(4) *Trouble* (1.18) (a) annoyance (b) nuisance (c) problem .

(5) *Apart from* (1.23) (a) as well as (b) except for (c) separated from

(6) *Hardly* (1.29) (a) hard (b) with difficulty (c) only just

(7) *Avoid* (1.31) (a) run away from (b) keep out of the way of (c) overtake

(8) *Reached* (1.36) (a) arrived in (b) achieved (c) approached

(9) *Awarded* (1.40) (a) promised (b) honoured (c) given

(10) *Nearly* (1.42) (a) hardly (b) almost (c) just over

C   Patterns

Study the pattern in italics in each case and then reproduce it, substituting the words given but taking care to form the verbs correctly. Change or put in articles, possessives, prepositions where necessary.

(1) *The people who lined the route did not realise how powerful cars had become in a few years*
   (a) man / sell / house / realise / valuable / property / become / a short time
   (b) girl / buy / ticket / realise / expensive / flights / become / the past year
   (c) man / return / abroad / imagine / much / children/grow/two years
   (d) people / come back / war / know / much / country/change/six years

(2) *There had already been several national championships* (of France) *before this one*
   (a) She/take part in/motor races/before the 1903 Grand Prix
   (b) There/be/crashes/when the race was stopped
   (c) He/win/prizes/before his victory in Bordeaux
   (d) He/publish/novels/before his name became well known

(3) *Madame du Gast, who had been keeping up with the leaders, lost two hours while she took care of him*
   (a) The Government,/worry about the accidents,/ stop race/ when the drivers reach Bordeaux
   (b) The Spanish crowds,/expect the drivers,/ go home/ when they hear the news
   (c) My father,/study in Paris,/teach French/when he return to England
   (d) Lucy,/wait for the letter,/tremble with excitement while she open it

(4) *The organisers had agreed that the race would be run from Paris to Madrid*
  (a) The company/decide/head office/transfer/London/Manchester
  (b) The pilot/announce/plane/divert/Orly/Heathrow
  (c) The teacher/say/examinations/hold/1 June/4 June
  (d) The police/state/prisoner/move/Wormwood Scrubs/Albany

(5) *By the time the drivers reached Bordeaux, the number of accidents had risen*
  (a) Madame du Gast/get to/Bordeaux/several other drivers/arrive
  (b) he/reach/cinema/the main film/begin
  (c) he/reach/home/several firemen/arrive
  (d) he/publish/book/similar books/appear

D Have Something Done (Get something done)

Local authorities did not usually have the roads surfaced with asphalt
The newspapers had begun a campaign to have the race stopped
Complete the sentences, using the correct form of the verb *have* and the past participle of the verb in brackets.

(1) He's going to .... (cut hair)
(2) She .... (repair car) yesterday.
only have → (3) I .... just .... (take out tooth)
(4) I'm going to .... (type letter) tomorrow morning.
" → (5) You look nice. Have you .... (do hair)?
(6) I must .... (renew driving licence)
(7) You can .... (take photograph) here.
(8) Next time, George is going to .... (paint kitchen).

E Preposition and Gerund

Now there were cars that were capable of going much faster
Complete the sentences with an appropriate verb in the gerund form.

→ (1) We look forward to (hearing) .... from you.
(2) I was turning over in my mind the idea of .... the *breaking* door down when the old lady appeared.

shutting (locking)

(3) He went out without .... the door.

(4) The competitors had to pay an entrance fee before
taking part in the race.

(5) He is a salesman so he is used to .... *travelling* about the
country in his job.

F Raise and Rise

Complete the sentences, using one of these verbs in the
correct form.

(1) The cars .... *raised* clouds of dust as they went by.

(2) By the time the drivers reached Bordeaux the number
of accidents had *risen*

(3) The sun always *rises* in the east.

(4) *Raise* your hand if you want to ask a question.

(5) The cost of living has *risen* by 10 per cent since last
year. *(en)*

(6) We are selling flags to *raise* .... money for the blind.

(7) We watched the balloon *rising* in the sky.

(8) The number of accidents *had risen* .... so quickly that the
newspapers began a campaign to have the race
stopped.

G Arrive and Reach

Rewrite the sentences, using *arrive* and the correct preposition, where one is necessary.

(1) By the time the drivers reached *arrived in* Bordeaux, the
number of accidents had risen.

(2) I reached the station half an hour late. *arrive*

(3) After such a long journey, he was glad to reach home.

(4) She has reached an age when she should be able to
look after herself.

(5) The committee took a long time to reach a decision.
arrive at

H Composition

You started to drive to a seaside town one Saturday.
When you were half-way there (a) you realised that you
had left your lunch basket at home (b) you overtook a

friend whose car had broken down (c) you saw that you had forgotten to put petrol in the tank and could not see a garage. Describe what you did in one of these situations.

PROGRESS TEST
Choose the correct alternative in each case.

By the time Madame du Gast $\frac{reached}{arrived}$ Bordeaux most of the other drivers $\frac{were\ already\ reached.}{had\ already\ arrived.}$ She $\frac{had\ been}{was}$ driving for several hours and at first $\frac{was\ keeping}{had\ been\ keeping}$ up with the leaders but she $\frac{must\ have\ stopped}{had\ had\ to\ stop}$ to look $\frac{for}{after}$ a driver and $\frac{his}{her}$ mechanic, who $\frac{had\ been\ hurt.}{were\ being\ hurt.}$ She was the $\frac{only}{unique}$ woman who $\frac{had\ entered\ in}{entered\quad for}$ the race and even her friends had not expected that she $\frac{would}{will}$ win. They $\frac{had\ told\ her}{were\ telling\ her}$ that she would crash and $\frac{would}{will}$ have to $\frac{have\ her\ car\ repaired.}{repair\ her\ car.}$ But her hopes of $\frac{winning}{win}$ had been $\frac{raising}{rising}$ during the race until she saw the other driver $\frac{to\ crash}{crash}$ and it was only because of her kindness that she lost so much time.

8 How to Win Friends and Sell Records

It is Angela's first day as an assistant in a record shop. She is nervous and not looking forward to it. Luckily, Judy, a much more experienced girl, is there to guide her.

ANGELA		What shall I do if <u>I get into difficulties?</u>
5	JUDY	Don't worry. I'll be here if you need me. But *if you keep calm, everything will be all right.* If a customer doesn't remember the name of a record or an artist, look it up in the catalogue; *if you don't know where a record is kept, ask me;* if we haven't got a record in stock, try to interest him in a different one.
10		
	ANGELA	*If I knew as much about music as you do, I would be* much more *confident.*
	JUDY	You're talking to me as if I were an expert.
15	ANGELA	You sound like an expert to me.
	JUDY	I know more about selling records than I do about music. But if you had worked here for three years, like me, you would have learnt where everything is. Look out! Here comes a customer.
20		
	ANGELA	Good morning, madam. What can I do for you?
	CUSTOMER	I'm looking for a record for my husband.
	ANGELA	Have you any particular record in mind?
	CUSTOMER	Yes. He was listening to some music on the radio last night, which he liked very much.
25		
	ANGELA	Do you remember the title?
	CUSTOMER	No. Now *I wish I had written it down. If I had, I wouldn't have forgotten it.*
	ANGELA	Well, what sort of music does your husband like best?
30		
	CUSTOMER	He likes all kinds. If he were here, he would be able to tell you. But I want the record to be a surprise, you see.
	ANGELA	Oh dear! *I wish I knew what to recommend. If I knew, I'd suggest something,* but . . .
35		
	JUDY	(who has been looking on all the time, amused) Did you say this music was on the radio last night, madam?
	CUSTOMER	Yes. About half-past nine.
40	JUDY	Half-past nine? Then it must have been Beethoven's Eroica symphony. They were broadcasting it from Germany.
	CUSTOMER	I expect that was it. I'll take it if you have it in stock.

45	JUDY	Certainly, madam. I think you'll find this is the best recording. If your husband isn't satisfied, we'll be pleased to exchange it for any record in the same price range. (she wraps up the record and the customer goes out)
50	ANGELA	I was looking to you for help. But how did you know that that was the record her husband heard last night?
	JUDY	I didn't. It would have been a miracle if I had even guessed it. But *if I hadn't said anything, she*
55		*would have gone away* and we wouldn't have sold a record! You'll soon learn. But in this business, *if you don't take a chance, you never sell anything.*

A Comprehension

Which of the following statements is correct in the context of the passage?

(1) If a customer doesn't know the name of an artist, Angela must (a) give him a catalogue (b) try to find it in the catalogue (c) ask Judy.

(2) Judy (a) knows a lot about music (b) is a very experienced sales girl (c) would have learnt about music if she had worked in the shop for three years.

(3) The customer (a) knows which record she wants (b) will accept any record (c) doesn't know the name of the record she wants.

(4) Judy interrupts (a) to make Angela look foolish (b) because she knows which record the customer wants (c) because she wants to help Angela and sell a record.

(5) If the customer's husband doesn't like the record she has bought (a) he can come back and buy something else (b) he can exchange it for a different recording of the Eroica symphony (c) he can exchange it for another record at a similar price.

B Words

Choose the word or phrase from the alternatives given

which is closest in meaning to the words in italics in the context of the passage.

(1) *Nervous* (1.2) (a) excited (b) afraid of what may happen (c) irritable
(2) *Artist* (1.8) (a) performer (b) actor (c) painter
(3) *I wish* (1.27) (a) if only (b) I desire (c) I want
(4) *Looking on* (1.36) (a) watching, without taking part (b) regarding (c) overseeing
(5) *In the same price range* (1.48) (a) varying in price to the same extent (b) which has won the same awards (c) costing about the same amount of money

C Patterns

Study the pattern in italic type in each case and then reproduce it, substituting the words given but taking care to form the verbs correctly. Change or put in articles, possessives, prepositions where necessary.

(1a) *If you keep calm, everything will be all right*
    (a) seem confident/the customers/impressed
    (b) look interested /the teacher/happy
    (c) work hard/the boss/satisfied

(1b) *If you don't know where a record is kept, ask me*
    (a) know/if/record/in stock/look it up
    (b) remember/how/word/spell/ask the teacher
    (c) understand/how/tax form/fill in/get an accountant

(1c) *If you don't take a chance, you never sell anything*
    (a) take/notes/remember
    (b) read/books/learn
    (c) listen to/people/understand

(2a) *If I knew as much about music as you do, I would be confident*
    (a) earn/money/he/I/rich
    (b) work/hours/they/I/exhausted
    (c) sell/records/Judy/satisfied

(2b) *I wish I knew what to recommend. If I knew, I'd suggest something*
    (a) how/mend the radio/fix it

(b) where/buy the book/get it this afternoon

(c) whether/exchange the record/take it back

(3a) *If I hadn't said anything, she would have gone away*

(a) suggest/the customer/leave

(b) sell/Judy/laugh

(c) buy/my wife/complain

(3b) *I wish I had written it down. If I had, I wouldn't have forgotten it*

(a) lock up/the burglar/get in

(b) give back/I/lose it

(c) turn off/the heater/blow up

D What to Do

Angela didn't know what to recommend

This pattern can be used instead of 'Angela didn't know what she should (ought to) recommend'.

Complete the sentences with the appropriate question word – *how, how much, what, whether, where, which, who.*

(1) He didn't know .... to repair it.

(2) She didn't know .... recording of the Eroica symphony to choose.

(3) They were looking for a record shop so I told them .... to go and .... to get there.

(4) I was so surprised that I didn't know .... to say.

(5) He didn't know .... to pay for the record.

(6) She doesn't know .... to go home or not.

(7) I don't know .... to invite to the party.

(8) I don't know .... to give him for his birthday present.

E As and Like (2)

(1) *You're talking to me as if I were an expert. You sound like an expert*

Use the words supplied to imitate this pattern in the following sentences.

(a) He's/speak to them/they/children./They behave

(b) He's/point at you/you/criminal/I feel

(c) They're/look after her/she/princess/She looks

(2) *Famous drivers like Marcel Renault, Bugatti and Lancia took part in the race*

Use the words supplied to imitate this pattern in the following sentences.

(a) actors/Burt Lancaster, Kirk Douglas and Tony Curtis/film
(b) players/Pele, Eusebio and Charlton/game
(c) artists/Manet, Monet and Renoir/exhibition

(3) The second example could be rewritten:
Such famous drivers as Marcel Renault, Bugatti and Lancia took part in the race

Rewrite your answers to (2), substituting *such .... as* for *like*.

F Phrasal Verbs – Look

Complete the sentences with one of the following prepositions – *after, down on, for, forward to, into, on, out, over, to, up.*

(1) I am looking *for.* my record player. Have you seen it anywhere?
(2) She has been looking *forward to* .... her holidays since last summer.
(3) I'll look *after* the children for you while you are out.
(4) If you don't know the name of the artist, look it *up*. in the catalogue.
(5) I looked *to*.. her for advice when I was in trouble.
(6) I didn't take part in the argument. I just looked *on*.
(7) Look *out*.! There's a car coming.
(8) She looks *down on* .... us because she belongs to an exclusive club.
(9) I'd like to look *over* the house before deciding whether to buy it.
(10) I'll look *into* your complaint, madam, and find out what went wrong.

G Composition

(1) If you were offered a free ticket to any country in the

world, where would you go and what would you expect to see there?

(2) Last week you filled in a football pools coupon. The first prize was £50,000. Unfortunately, you did not win. What would you have done with the money if you had won?

(3) You intended to go on holiday with a friend. At the last minute he/she could not go with you. Write a postcard saying that you are sorry he/she is missing what you are enjoying.

PROGRESS TEST

Choose the correct alternative in each case.

If I have another customer $\frac{\text{like}}{\text{as}}$ that lady I $\frac{\text{will go}}{\text{am going}}$ mad.

I wish I $\frac{\text{know}}{\text{knew}}$ as much about records $\frac{\text{like}}{\text{as}}$ Judy. I would have been embarrassed if she $\frac{\text{would not have}}{\text{had not}}$ come to help. Still, if I had worked in the shop $\frac{\text{for}}{\text{since}}$ three years I $\frac{\text{would have}}{\text{had}}$ learnt how $\frac{\text{to deal}}{\text{I am dealing}}$ with customers. If the lady's husband $\frac{\text{doesn't}}{\text{won't}}$ like the record he will probably bring it back. It $\frac{\text{will}}{\text{would}}$ be funny if he hated Beethoven but perhaps it would be awkward for Judy if he $\frac{\text{would come}}{\text{came}}$ back and $\frac{\text{complained.}}{\text{would complain.}}$ Here comes $\frac{\text{another}}{\text{other}}$ customer. I am not $\frac{\text{looking forward}}{\text{looking for}}$ to serving him. I must $\frac{\text{remember}}{\text{remind}}$ Judy's advice: 'If you keep calm, everything $\frac{\text{would be}}{\text{will be}}$ all right. If you $\frac{\text{don't know}}{\text{aren't knowing}}$ where a record is kept, look $\frac{\text{it up}}{\text{for it}}$ in the catalogue. If you $\frac{\text{aren't taking}}{\text{don't take}}$ a chance, you never sell anything.

9 Castle of Dreams

On the coast of California, on top of a mountain, stands
an enormous castle which looks as if it has been lifted
out of the Middle Ages and laid on the site. In fact the
castle, called San Simeon, was built for the American
5 newspaper proprietor, William Randolph Hearst, but it is
furnished with objects dating from different historical
periods, which were transported from Europe.

It took thirty years to build the castle and even then it
was never completed. Throughout this time, over a
10 hundred workmen were permanently employed on the
site and the architect, Julia Morgan, was continually
obliged to change the design, as often as Hearst changed
his mind. Rooms and whole *floors were constructed but then
had to be knocked down* and rebuilt to please him.

15 Agents were sent all over Europe to find works of art
to decorate the castle. Old ceilings and fireplaces,
furniture, paintings and statues were purchased and
shipped to America. *An enormous number of objects were
bought but many of them could not be used* and were stored in
20 warehouses, some of them not even unpacked.

Hearst's life was used as the basis for Orson Welles's
film 'Citizen Kane'. Kane, who was meant to stand for
Hearst, built a fantastic castle like San Simeon, but in the
film it was called Xanadu, the name being taken from the
25 name of the dream palace in a famous poem by Coleridge.

Since Hearst's death *San Simeon has been turned into a
tourist attraction and the possessions* which lay untouched in
warehouses *are* gradually *being sold. The castle has been
handed over to the American people and* eventually *the contents
30 will also be given to them.* Unfortunately, they are not worth
very much. Hearst's agents were often deceived by art
dealers, who sold them cheap imitations instead of real
works of art.

A Comprehension

Which of the following statements is correct in the context
of the passage?

   (1) The castle of San Simeon (a) was transported from Europe (b) was furnished with works of art from Europe (c) was built by William Randolph Hearst.

   (2) It took a long time to build the castle because (a) only a hundred workmen were employed on it (b) it was badly designed (c) the owner did not know what he wanted.

   (3) A large number of works of art bought for the castle were not used because (a) Hearst did not like them (b) there was not enough room for them (c) they were stored in warehouses.

   (4) The castle in 'Citizen Kane' was called Xanadu because (a) Orson Welles thought it was a poetic name (b) he didn't want people to know he was referring to San Simeon (c) Hearst's idea of building such a fantastic castle reminded him of a poem.

   (5) The contents of San Simeon (a) still belong to Hearst's family (b) now belong to the American people (c) are kept in warehouses.

B Words

Choose the word or phrase from the alternatives given which is closest in meaning to the words in italics in the context of the passage.

   (1) *On the coast* (1.1) (a) on the beach (b) near the sea (c) on the shore.

   (2) *Continually* (1.11) (a) repeatedly (b) continuously (c) usually.

   (3) *Whole floors* (1.13) (a) all the floors (b) all the rooms on a floor (c) complete flats.

   (4) *Agents* (1.15) (a) officials (b) inspectors (c) representatives.

   (5) *Purchased* (1.17) (a) bought (b) sold (c) exchanged.

   (6) *Stand for* (1.22) (a) represent (b) take the place of (c) be in favour of.

   (7) *Famous* (1.25) (a) known (b) well known (c) notorious.

   (8) *Handed over* (1.29) (a) sold (b) given (c) offered.

   (9) *Eventually* (1.29) (a) in fact (b) gradually (c) in time.

   (10) *They are not worth very much* (1.30) (a) they are cheap (b) they have little value (c) they are useless.

C Patterns

Study the pattern in italic type in each case and then reproduce it, substituting the words given but taking care to form the verbs correctly. Change or put in articles, possessives, prepositions where necessary.

(1) *San Simeon has been turned into a tourist attraction and the possessions are being sold*
   (a) The book/adapt to/film/film/make.
   (b) His house/preserve as/museum/art collection/put on show.
   (c) The land/buy for/housing estate/trees/cut down.

(2) *The castle has been handed over to the American people and the contents will also be given to them*
   (a) The paintings/present/National Gallery/the sculptures/later/offer/the people.
   (b) A plan/submit/the management/a report/eventually /send/them. *set out*
   (c) A complaint/send/the authorities/the evidence/later/forward to/them.

(3) *Floors were constructed but then had to be knocked down*
   (a) Objects/buy/store.
   (b) Copies/publish/withdraw. *wiθdrɔ: (retirar)*
   (c) Invitations/send out/cancel.

(4) *An enormous number of objects were bought but many of them could not be used*
   (a) large number/people/rescue/many/save.
   (b) large amount/money/recover/much/account for.
   (c) great deal/work/do/much/justify.

D Active and Passive

Change the verbs in the passage below from passive to active. Begin 'William Randolph Hearst . . . . . '
Julia Morgan was chosen to design San Simeon by William Randolph Hearst, but she was continually ordered by him to change things; she was told to knock down whole floors which had been constructed by the workmen and <u>was made to rebuild</u> them. Agents were

sent by Hearst to find works of art for the castle which were shipped back by them to America. Since Hearst's death the castle has been given to the American people by his family and the contents will eventually be handed over by them. Unfortunately Hearst's agents were often deceived by art dealers and were sold cheap imitations by them instead of real works of art.

di'si:vd
(engañar)

Compare the form of the verb here ('was made to') to 'make and let' (Lesson 5(D))

E It Takes . . .

It took thirty years to build the castle
It took me a long time to finish the job

It takes can be used with or without the object form of the personal pronoun (*me, him, us* etc) in this construction, usually with an expression of time.

Complete the sentences, using the past tense and the words supplied.

(1) me/half an hour/get/station.
(2) her/two hours/get ready/party.
(3) him/a long time/answer/question.
(4) How long/you/sell/house?   } __ *did it take* ^you^ ___ ?
(5) How long/them/reply to/letter? }   *them*

F Lie and Lay

Fill in the blanks with the correct form of either the verb *lie* (lay, lain) or *lay* (laid, laid).

(1) The castle looks as if it has been lifted out of the Middle Ages and *laid* . on the site.
(2) The hen has *laid* . an egg.
(3) I have a headache. I'm going to *lie* . down.
(4) These paintings have *lain* untouched in the warehouse for years.
(5) She helped her mother to *lay* . the table.
(6) The book is *lying* . on the table.
(7) We have *laid* off 100 workmen because there is not enough for them to do.
→ (8) Hearst could not decide how the castle should be. . *lay* out.

lay out = disponer, repartir, organizar
(share out)

(9) The town where I live *lies* at the foot of a mountain.
(10) The Trade Union (have *been laid* the blame for the strike on the management.

σ : *The blame has been laid to the TU for the ---*

G Composition

Describe (a) your ideal house and how it would be laid out (b) how any typical product of your country is made (c) how Hearst's Castle was furnished.

PROGRESS TEST
Choose the correct alternative in each case.

'Citizen Kane' $\frac{\text{was made}}{\text{has been made}}$ in 1941. $\frac{\text{At}}{\text{In}}$ that time it was unusual for Hollywood directors $\frac{\text{to be allowed}}{\text{being allowed}}$ much freedom but Orson Welles $\frac{\text{was given}}{\text{gave}}$ the $\frac{\text{opportunity}}{\text{occasion}}$ to work in his own way. His reputation for originality $\frac{\text{had been established}}{\text{was being established}}$ three years earlier during a broadcast of 'The War of the Worlds'. $\frac{\text{On}}{\text{In}}$ that occasion large numbers of people $\frac{\text{had been convinced}}{\text{have been convinced}}$ that the world $\frac{\text{was being invaded}}{\text{was invading}}$ by creatures from Mars.

'Citizen Kane' $\frac{\text{has been shown}}{\text{is being shown}}$ all over the world and $\frac{\text{was once voting}}{\text{was once voted}}$ the greatest film ever $\frac{\text{done.}}{\text{made.}}$ In the film, Kane's life and career $\frac{\text{are reconstructed}}{\text{is reconstructed}}$ through flashbacks and Americans $\frac{\text{must have been reminded}}{\text{must have been remembered}}$ of William Randolph Hearst. But the main interest in the film $\frac{\text{lies}}{\text{lays}}$ in its original technique, which $\frac{\text{has since been used}}{\text{is since being used}}$ by $\frac{\text{other}}{\text{another}}$ directors. This is why the film $\frac{\text{is still being shown}}{\text{was still being shown}}$

in cinemas and why it $\dfrac{\text{will probably be remembered}}{\text{will probably be reminded}}$ when

Hearst himself $\dfrac{\text{has been forgotten.}}{\text{will be forgotten.}}$

10 Anyone for Tennis?

MICHAEL   Hello, Jean. I'm going to the club this afternoon. Would you like to play a mixed doubles?

JEAN   No, I'm sorry. I'd rather not play today. It's not that I don't like playing with you but I'm worn
5   out. I had to play a match against Catherine in the club tournament yesterday and I haven't got over it yet. My legs are still aching. So I'd
→ rather leave it <u>for</u> another day. I hope you don't mind me saying 'no'.

10 MICHAEL   No, that's all right. How did you get on in the match? Did you win?

JEAN   Yes, I managed to beat her in the end but I didn't enjoy playing. It started to rain half-way through the game and I can't stand playing in
15   the rain. I suggested going on with the match today, but she had arranged to go out with Fred so she persuaded me to continue.

MICHAEL   But you won all the same.

JEAN   Yes. I made her run about a lot. But I really won
20   because <u>she was conscious of Fred watching her</u> and he kept giving her pieces of advice. In the end she allowed <u>things to get on her nerves</u> and lost her temper. When we had finished playing she refused to speak to Fred.

25 MICHAEL   I've heard that she doesn't like being beaten. But if you want to win tennis matches you mustn't let things get you down.

JEAN   Fred said that he was only trying to help but she

5. 3. 33
(Pract. Engl. Usage)

at the end (of the year)
in the end (finally)

30   was so angry that she (still) hadn't forgiven him
when I left. I expect he'll get round her by
taking her with him on the car rally on Sunday
unless she's already been invited by someone
else. But perhaps she won't want to have anything to do with him any more. By the way,
35   have you put your name down for the rally yet?

MICHAEL Yes, I've already entered. But I need someone to
act as navigator. Would you like to come?

JEAN   I'd love to.

MICHAEL Right. What time shall I call for you? About ten?

40 JEAN   You'd better come about nine. All the cars are
supposed to set out from the club at 9.15.

MICHAEL What! I didn't realise we had to start as early
as that.

JEAN   (laughing) Do you still find it difficult to get up
45   in the morning?

MICHAEL On Sunday mornings, yes.

JEAN   Would you like me to ring you about eight?

MICHAEL Yes, please. And you'd better ring again at ten
past, just to make sure I'm up.

50 JEAN   OK, then. See you Sunday. Thanks for ringing.

I find it difficult to learn a language
learning a language difficult

A Comprehension

Which of the following statements is correct in the
context of the passage?

(1) Jean didn't accept Michael's invitation to play
tennis because (a) she didn't like mixed doubles
(b) she was too tired (c) she had already arranged
a match with someone else

(2) Catherine persuaded Jean to finish the match
because (a) she didn't mind playing in the rain
(b) she had arranged to go out with her boy-friend
the next day (c) she was winning

(3) After the match, Catherine refused to speak to
Fred because (a) he had given her bad advice
(b) she had lost her temper (c) he didn't want to go
out with her

(4) Jean (a) persuaded Michael to enter for the car

C

rally (b) asked if she could go with him as navigator
(c) was looking forward to the car rally
(5) Jean offered to telephone Michael on Sunday
(a) to tell him what time the rally was going to start
(b) to make sure he got up in time (c) to tell him
what time to call for her

B Words

Choose the word or phrase from the alternatives given
which is closest in meaning to the words in italics in the
context of the passage.

(1) *Worn out* (1.4) (a) used up (b) exhausted (c) depressed
(2) *Got over* (1.7) (a) recovered from (b) finished (c)
overtaken
(3) *Mind* (1.9) (a) think about (b) worry about (c) object
to
(4) *All the same* (1.18) (a) on equal terms (b) fairly (c)
nevertheless
(5) *Get you down* (1.27) (a) put you on the ground (b)
(b) depress you (c) frighten you

C Patterns

(1) Would you like to *play tennis* this afternoon?
I'd rather *play* tomorrow. I like *playing tennis* but I
want to finish *writing some letters*. But I'd love *to play*
another day.
Repeat the pattern of the conversation, replacing the
words in italic type with the following:
(a) go to the zoo/go/going to the zoo/decorating my
room/ to go
(b) go shopping/go/going shopping/doing my home-
work/to go
(c) go out with me/go out/going out with you/
typing my lecture notes/to go out.

(2) Jean's father refused to let her *go out with Michael.*
She kept asking him why he wouldn't *allow her to go
out with him* but he didn't want to tell her. Then she
tried to persuade him to *change his mind.* In the end
he said that *Michael should have his hair cut.*

Repeat the pattern of the conversation, as above:

(a) leave home/give her a reason/reconsider/she should wait until she was eighteen

(b) have a motor-cycle/agree to this/think again/ she should learn to ride a bicycle first

(c) marry Michael/give his permission/be more reasonable/Michael should earn his own living

(3) Jean arranged to meet Michael *at the zoo*. He made her wait a long time and she started *to get angry*. When he arrived, *the zoo had already closed* so he suggested *going to a restaurant* instead. She didn't mind *going to a restaurant* but said he had better *buy a watch*.

Repeat the pattern of the conversation, as above:

(a) at the cinema/to get annoyed/the film had already started/having a drink/having a drink/ come earlier next time

(b) at the station/to lose her temper/the train had already left/going by bus/going by bus/buy a timetable

(c) at the theatre/to get worried/the seats had already been sold/going dancing/going dancing/buy the tickets in advance next time

D   Gerund as Object

I hope you don't mind my saying 'no'
She was conscious of Fred's watching her
These sentences can be rewritten, using the objective form instead of the possessive form, and <u>the objective form is much more common:</u>
I hope you don't mind me saying 'no'
She was conscious of Fred watching her
In the following sentences, change the possessive form to the objective – for example, *my* to *me*.

(1) The rain didn't stop *our* playing.   (us)
(2) She didn't like *Michael's* getting up late.   (Michael)
(3) I remember *your* pulling up the weeds.   (you)
(4) He can't understand *my* taking so long to get ready.   (me)
(5) We're afraid of *their* missing their train.   (them)

E   Had Better

What time shall I call for you? About ten?

You'd better come about nine. All the cars are supposed to set out from the club at 9.15.

Had better means 'it would be more to (my, your etc.) advantage if (I, you, etc.) . . . ' or 'it would be a good idea if . . . '

Use the words in brackets to make sentences giving reasons for the sentences containing *had better*.

(1) You'd better take an umbrella. (sky cloudy)
(2) **We'**d better hurry. (train already in station)
(3) You'd better drive carefully. (ice on road)
(4) We'd better put her up for the night. (missed last bus)
(5) I'd better turn the gas off. (another explosion)

F   Would Rather

(1) *I'd rather not play today. I'd rather leave it for another day*
Repeat the pattern, substituting the words supplied.
    (a) do my homework/until tomorrow
    (b) mow the lawn/until next week
    (c) paint the kitchen/until the summer

(2) *Which would you rather have? Tea or coffee? I'd rather have coffee*
Repeat the pattern, choosing between the following alternatives:
    (a) a glass of milk/a glass of beer
    (b) a lot of money/a lot of friends
    (c) a house at the seaside/a house in the country

(3) *What would you rather do? Play tennis or go to the cinema? I'd rather play tennis*
Repeat the pattern, choosing between the following alternatives:
    (a) work in an office/work in a factory
    (b) listen to records/sing a song yourself
    (c) eat in a restaurant/eat at home

G   Still, Yet, Already, Not . . . any more

In each case, reproduce the pattern, using the words supplied.

(1a) *I haven't got over it yet. My legs are still aching*
    (a) They/finished the match/They/playing
    (b) She/forgiven Fred/They/arguing
    (c) You/answered my question/I/waiting

(1b) *Have you put your name down for the rally yet? Yes, I've already entered for it*
    (a) read the notes for this lesson/read them
    (b) got a navigator for the rally/asked Jean
    (c) telephoned Michael about the match/rung him

(1c) *Hasn't she forgiven him yet?*   *Has she forgiven him yet?*
    (i) *No, she's still arguing*   *only here*
    (ii) *Yes, she's already forgotten the argument*
    (a) they finished the match (i) playing
                       (ii) come off the court
    (b) he asked her to marry (i) thinking about it
        him   (ii) fixed the date
    (c) she left home   (i) living with her parents
                        (ii) moved in with some other girls

(2) *She was so angry that she still hadn't forgiven him when I left*
    (a) He/sleepy/he/got up/Jean rang again
    (b) The match/long/she/got over it/she played the next day
    (c) The exercise/difficult/I/finished it/the bell rang

(3a) *Does he still live in London? No, he doesn't live there any more but he still visits it occasionally*
    (a) have to work at the weekend?/work on Saturdays and Sundays/ works at night
    (b) play football and tennis?/play football/plays tennis
    (c) take part in car rallies?/drive in them/navigates

(3b) *Doesn't she go out with Fred any more?*
    (i) *Yes, they're still good friends*

    (ii) *No, they no longer get on very well*
    (a) she play tennis/   (i) she's/a good player
                            (ii) she/has the time
    (b) she go to Dr. Anderson (i) he's/the family doctor
                            (ii) he's/in practice here
    (c) she shop at Hardy's/   (i) they're/the best
                                  sports shop
                            (ii) they're/in business

H   Phrasal Verbs – Get

Complete the sentences with one of the following prepositions: *away, away with, down, on (3), on with, out of, over, up*

(1) I asked Johnny's teacher how he was getting .*on*. at school.
(2) I get .*up*. at seven o'clock every morning. *(with)*
(3) Don't sit there doing nothing. Get .*on*. your work.
(4) She was upset when she heard the news but now she has got .*over*. it.
(5) She had a bad temper when she was a little girl so we didn't get .*on*. very well.
(6) This terrible weather is getting me . . . .
(7) I ran after the thief but unfortunately he got .*away*.
(8) He kept asking me to go out with him. In the end, it got . . . . my nerves.
(9) You said that you would help me with the washing-up. Don't try to get . . . . it.
(10) I'm not going to punish you now, but next time I won't let you get . . . . it

Prepositions with Call

Complete the sentences with one of the following prepositions: *at (2), for, on (2)*

(1) I'll call .*for*. *(on)* you at eight thirty and we'll drive to the club.
(2) The postman called .*at*. *(in)* the house with a parcel.
(3) The Vicar calls .*on*. his parishioners from time to time.

call for → need sab hola

on : person

(4) I called *for* you ..*at* your office yesterday but you weren't there.

J Composition

Briefly explain (a) what you like doing most in your spare time (b) what you would like to do if you had enough money (c) what you hate having to do.

PROGRESS TEST
Put the verbs in brackets into the correct form (gerund or infinitive with or without *to*)
Michael doesn't like (dance). He would rather (go) to the cinema. But Jean enjoys (dance) so much that he let her (persuade) him (take) her to the club last Saturday. When they arrived, a lot of other young men wanted (dance) with her and kept (ask) her (go) on the floor with them. This made Michael (feel) jealous. He suggested (go) outside for a breath of air, but at that moment it started (rain). Jean began (get) annoyed. 'I know you hate (dance),' she said, 'but why should you (try) (stop) other people (dance)?' Michael thought he had better (dance) with her. He didn't want her (lose) her temper.

11 Father can't say 'No'

Mr. Bradford has just come home from the office one Friday evening. His son, Tom, aged 18, is in the sitting-room waiting for him.

TOM   Hello, Dad. How did things go at the

5   office today?

MR. BRADFORD (a little surprised at Tom's interest) Quite well. Nothing special happened. Is your mother in?

TOM   No. She went across the road half an hour

10		ago to borrow some sugar from Mrs. Davies. *Shall I go over and tell her you're home?*
	MR. BRADFORD	She'll be back soon, I expect. I wonder where she put my slippers.
15	TOM	She probably took them up to the bedroom, Dad. *Would you like me to fetch them for you?*
	MR. BRADFORD	(again surprised at Tom's concern for him) No, it's all right. Here they are.
	TOM	Dad, *will you do me a favour, please?*
	MR. BRADFORD	It depends what it is.
20	TOM	*May I borrow the car tomorrow night?*
	MR. BRADFORD	What's wrong with your motor-cycle? Has it broken down?
25	TOM	No, but I'm taking Janet to a party in Waterbury. It wouldn't be fair to ask her to sit on the back of the 'bike' in her party dress.
	MR. BRADFORD	What sort of party is it? There'll be plenty to drink, I suppose.
30	TOM	Oh yes, but that doesn't matter. Janet will drive the car home. She never drinks much at parties.
	MR. BRADFORD	*Can Janet drive?*
	TOM	*Yes, she can.* She passed her test last year.
35	MR. BRADFORD	That's very convenient. You ask me if you can borrow the car but Janet is going to drive it home. Hasn't *her* father got a car?
	TOM	Dad, I couldn't ask her to take me in her father's car.
40	MR. BRADFORD	Why not?
	TOM	She would have to come and fetch me. Her father wouldn't like that.
	MR. BRADFORD	But he wouldn't mind if she brought you home in *my* car, I suppose.
45	TOM	He wouldn't know. I'd take her home on foot once we arrived here. It's not far to her house.
50	MR. BRADFORD	May I ask you something, Tom? What do you think your grandfather would have said if I'd asked him if I could borrow his

car to take your mother out and told him
she would drive me home?

TOM He would have said 'no', I suppose. But
parents were much stricter in those days.
55 And anyway, *Mother couldn't drive, could she?*

MR. BRADFORD (realising that he has lost the argument)
No, she couldn't. Well, I'll lend you the car,
Tom, if you don't drink too much. Then
you can drive it home yourself.

60 TOM Thanks, Dad. *Can I telephone Janet and tell
her it's all right?*

MR. BRADFORD Yes, yes. But before you do, *would you
mind telling your mother I'm home?* I'm hungry.

A   Comprehension

Which of the following statements is correct in the context
of the passage?

(1) Tom (a) always shows great interest in his father's
work (b) thought that something important had
happened at the office (c) wanted to put his father in
a good humour.

(2) Tom can't take Janet to the party on his motor-cycle
because (a) it has broken down (b) she would not be
wearing suitable clothes (c) she is afraid of sitting on
the back of it.

(3) Tom and Janet can't go to the party in her father's
car because (a) she can't drive (b) her father would
probably not approve (c) her father doesn't like Tom.

(4) Janet's father (a) wouldn't mind if Janet drove Tom
home in Mr. Bradford's car (b) would think they
had walked to the party (c) would not know that
Janet had driven Tom home.

(5) Mr. Bradford finally (a) agrees to lend Tom the car
if he drives it home (b) agrees to let Janet drive
his car home (c) agrees to lend Tom the car only
if Janet drives it home.

B   Words

Choose the word or phrase from the alternatives given

which is closest in meaning to the words in italics in the context of the passage.

(1) *Shall I* (1.11) (a) will I (b) am I going to (c) would you like me to.
(2) *Plenty* (1.28) (a) a number (b) a lot (c) much.
(3) *Passed* (1.33) (a) approved (b) went by (c) was successful in.
(4) *Fetch* (1.41) (a) bring (b) carry (c) call for.
(5) *Far* (1.46) (a) a long way (b) a distance (c) long.

C Patterns

(1) *Shall I fetch your slippers for you?*
   Would you like me to fetch your slippers for you?
Rewrite the following sentences, substituting the alternative construction for the one used.
   (a) Shall I open the window?
   (b) Shall I write down the address for you?
   (c) Would you like me to hold the ladder for you?
   (d) Shall I post the letters?
   (e) Would you like me to go with you?

(2) *Will you do me a favour, please?*
   Would you mind doing me a favour?
As above, substitute the alternative construction for the one used.
   (a) Will you hold this for me, please?
   (b) Will you pay for the tickets in advance, please?
   (c) Would you mind closing the door?
   (d) Will you lend me five pounds, please?
   (e) Would you mind repeating the question?

(3) *May/Can I borrow the car tomorrow night?*
   Might/Could I borrow the car tomorrow night?
Rewrite the following sentences, using the more polite form.
   (a) May I ask you something?
   (b) Can I answer the questions in pencil?
   (c) May I use your telephone?
   (d) Can I come into the office half an hour late tomorrow?
   (e) May I leave the class ten minutes early?

(4) *Can Janet drive a car? Yes, she can.*
Could she drive a car two years ago? No, she couldn't.

Answer the following questions and then put question and answer into the past tense, using the words in brackets.

    (a) Can you swim? .... (when you were five years old)
    (b) Can you speak English? .... (ten years ago)
    (c) Can you ride a bicycle? .... (when you were a child)
    (d) Can you type? .... (five years ago)
    (e) Can you read music? .... (when you were at school)

D   Bring, take, fetch

Choose the correct verb to fill the blanks in the following sentences and put it in the correct form.

    (1) Mother probably .... your slippers upstairs, Dad. Shall I .... them for you?
    (2) I am .... Janet to a party in Waterbury tomorrow night.
    (3) I'll .... Janet to the party and she'll .... me home.
    (4) I forgot to .... my books to class today. I've left them at home.
    (5) I've left the papers in my office. Wait here for me while I .... them.
    (6) Look, Mother! Tom has .... you some flowers.
    (7) Don't leave me here alone. .... me with you.
    (8) Mother's over the road talking to Mrs. Davies. Shall I go and .... her?
    (9) He hasn't returned the books he borrowed. If he doesn't .... them back tomorrow, I'll have to go and .... them.
    (10) Waiter, this soup is cold. .... it away and .... me some fruit juice instead.

E   Borrow and Lend

May I borrow the car?
She went to borrow some sugar from Mrs. Davies
I'll lend you the car

Mrs Davies lent some sugar to her
Study these constructions and then complete the sentences
with the correct form of one of these verbs.

(1) 'Hello, Tom. Is your father going to....us the car
tomorrow?'
'Yes, He says we can...it. Of course, I've often...it
from him before but this time he didn't want to...it
to me. He wondered if your father would ... you *his*
car.'
'It's all right. Father will....me *his* providing *you*
drive me home. He trusts you, you see.'

(2) If you don't want to....me the money, I'll have to
....it from someone else. (Can the first part of the
sentence be written in a different way?).

F Pronunciation (2)

In each group of four words below, three words rhyme
but one does not. Choose the word that does not rhyme
with the others in the group.

(1) (a) worry	(b) hurry	(c) sorry	(d) curry
(2) (a) laid	(b) made	(c) said	(d) paid
(3) (a) fork	(b) talk	(c) work	(d) walk
(4) (a) throw	(b) grow	(c) allow	(d) owe
(5) (a) use(v)	(b) use(n)	(c) news	(d) shoes
(6) (a) heard	(b) word	(c) bird	(d) sword
(7) (a) cut	(b) shut	(c) but	(d) put
(8) (a) says	(b) raise	(c) days	(d) phrase
(9) (a) prize	(b) cries	(c) buys	(d) ice
(10) (a) won	(b) done	(c) gone	(d) sun

G Composition

Using the text as a model, write a short dialogue (a)
asking your father if you can borrow the car (b) asking a
friend if you can borrow his typewriter (c) asking your
father if you can go to a week-end party in another town.

PROGRESS TEST
(A) Rewrite the following sentences to express the same
meaning in a different way.

(1) Shall I go with you?

(2) Would you like me to close the door?

(3) Will you repeat the question, please?

(4) Would you mind lending me five pounds?

(B) Choose the correct alternative in each case.

Tom $\frac{could}{might}$ ride a motor-cycle when he was seventeen.

He had $\frac{already \quad passed}{yet \quad approved}$ the test for motor-cycles

before he learnt to $\frac{drive}{conduct}$ a car. His father $\frac{borrowed}{lent}$

him his car for the test but $\frac{took}{brought}$ him to the examina-

tion centre and went to $\frac{take}{fetch}$ him $\frac{afterwards.}{after}$ Tom passed

the test and then $\frac{said: \ 'Shall \ I \ lend}{told: \ 'Could \ I \ borrow}$ the car again this

evening, Dad?'

12 You may be Disappointed

Two girls are waiting outside a cinema.

BARBARA Do you think those two boys have forgotten
that they were supposed to meet us here at
eight o'clock?

CHRISTINE They'll probably be here soon. Perhaps they
5 can't find the cinema.

BARBARA Nonsense! Everyone knows where the ABC is.
Of course, *they may not come* at all. *They may never
have intended to turn up.* We've only met them
once, so for all we know *they may be sitting in a*
10 *pub* having a drink.

CHRISTINE *They can't be.* They sounded so keen at the 'disco' last Saturday. You know, *you can be very suspicious at times,* Barbara.

BARBARA And you can be very naive. *They may have asked us out just to see if we'd say 'yes'!*

15

CHRISTINE There may be a simple explanation. *Their car may have broken down.* They might even have had an accident.

BARBARA They *might* have. But John hasn't got a car.

20 CHRISTINE Peter *has.* He's got a red Mini.

BARBARA That's something in his favour. At least he may take us both home afterwards. Look at the time! It's a quarter past eight. We can't wait much longer.

25 CHRISTINE What shall we do, then?

BARBARA We may as well go in and see the film. It would be a pity to miss it after all this waiting.

CHRISTINE Look, there's a red Mini! Oh dear, now it's gone past. I thought it might have been Peter's.

30 BARBARA Come on, Christine! *Let's go in! I've had enough of this.*

CHRISTINE Not yet. That car may have been Peter's. They may be looking for a place to park.

(John and Peter arrive)

35 PETER I'm sorry we're late. You haven't been waiting long, have you?

BARBARA Eighteen and a half minutes.

JOHN We had a lot of trouble on the way. First, Peter couldn't start the car. Then we had to stop at

40 the garage for some petrol, because we thought we might not have enough for the journey home. Then *we couldn't find anywhere to park but in the end we were able to squeeze into a gap* just round the corner.

45 BARBARA Well, better late than never.

CHRISTINE *Shall we go inside? The film may have started.*

PETER No, it can't have. The feature film doesn't start until nine. We've time to have some coffee. That way we can really get to know you two.

50 CHRISTINE OK. Let's go, then.

BARBARA As I said before, Christine, you can be very naive

at times. But don't offer to buy the coffee. They might accept.

A   Comprehension

Which of the following statements is correct in the context of the passage?

(1) Barbara thinks John and Peter may not come because (a) they drink a lot (b) they may never have intended to meet the girls (c) the girls were not sure what time they were supposed to meet them.

(2) Christine doesn't agree with Barbara because (a) she is naive (b) she is suspicious of her (c) she thinks the boys were very interested in meeting them again.

(3) Christine (a) believes John and Peter have had an accident (b) thinks it is just possible that they have had an accident (c) knows that they have had an accident.

(4) Barbara is pleased to hear that Peter has a car because (a) she hopes he will take her home (b) she likes Minis (c) she only likes men with cars.

(5) The boys arrived late because (a) they had an accident (b) they had a lot of difficulties on the way (c) they forgot about the meeting.

B   Words

Choose the word or phrase from the alternatives given which is closest in meaning to the words in italics in the context of the passage.

(1) *Intended* (1.8) (a) expected (b) tried (c) meant

(2) *Naive* (1.14) (a) innocent (b) stupid (c) native

(3) *Asked us out* (1.14) (a) told us to go outside (b) asked if they could meet us outside (c) invited us to go out with them

(4) *To miss it* (1.27) (a) to lose it (b) not to see it (c) not to find it

(5) *Gap* (1.43) (a) space (b) hole (c) entrance

C   Patterns

Study the pattern in italic type in each case and then

reproduce it, substituting the words given but taking care to form the verbs correctly. Change or put in articles, possessives, prepositions where necessary.

(1) *They may be sitting in a pub. But they may not be. They may be on their way to the cinema*
    (a) He/work/office/he/He/on his way home
    (b) She/type/letters/she/She/speak to the boss
    (c) He/repair/car/he/He/sell petrol

(2) *He may be in the pub. He can't be. He doesn't drink beer*
    (a) at the football match/like football
    (b) at the tennis club/belong to the club
    (c) in the library/like reading

(3) *They may not come. They might not come, but I think they will*
    (a) He/win/He/win/he
    (b) It/rain/It/rain/it
    (c) She/pass/She/pass/she

(4) *Their car may have broken down. It can't have done. It's only just been repaired*
    (a) The bridge/collapse/It/It's/build
    (b) He/resign/He/He's/appoint
    (c) The lights/fuse/They/They've/install

(5) *They may have asked us out just to see if we'd say 'yes'. They couldn't have done. That would have been silly*
    (a) He/drop it/it/break/He/That/ridiculous
    (b) He/take it back/they/change it/He/That/absurd
    (c) She/arrive late/the boss/notice/She/That/very risky

(6) *They may never have intended to turn up. They might not have done but they sounded very keen*
    (a) She/expect/pass/She/she/seem/confident
    (b) He/mean/enter/He/he/appear/interested
    (c) She/want/come/She/she/look/enthusiastic

(7) *Generally the weather is good but it can rain heavily at times*
    (a) you/trusting/you/be very suspicious
    (b) he/hard-working/he/be very lazy
    (c) she/good-natured/she/be very bad-tempered

D Could and Was Able To

When achievement is involved in a past action, we use
was able to in place of *could*, or substitute *managed to* or
succeeded in.
*We couldn't find anywhere to park but in the end we were able to
squeeze into a gap* (But compare Lesson 11, Pattern (4),
where *could* means 'knew how to').
When is it better to write *could* (*not*) and where is it necessary
to use the form *was able to* in the following passage?
The sailor . . . . see that the boat was going to hit the rocks
and so he . . . . jump into the sea before the shock came.
He . . . . swim very well so he . . . . reach a fishing boat not
far away. When the fishermen pulled him on board he . . . .
understand what they were saying at first because they
spoke Spanish but after a time he . . . . remember a few
words of their language and ask them for help. As their
boat was small they . . . . take it close to the rocks and so
they . . . . save the other members of the crew.

E Shall We? and Let's

Let's expresses the same idea as *shall we* more positively.
They are both ways of suggesting something: – *Shall we go
inside? The film may have started. Let's go in! I've had enough
of this.* Use these forms to complete the following sentences,
choosing the more appropriate expression in each case.

(1) . . . . wait a little longer. They may come after all.
(2) . . . . wait a little longer. I'm sure they'll be here soon.
(3) . . . . have coffee with them or would you rather go
     into the cinema?
(4) . . . . have coffee with them. There's plenty of time
     before the film starts.
(5) . . . . go to Italy for our holidays. It seems a very
     interesting country.
(6) . . . . go to Italy for our holidays. I'm sure we would
     have a wonderful time.

F Find, Meet, Get to Know, Know

Choose the correct verb to fill in the blanks in the following
sentences and put it in the correct form.

(1) I may go to....him at the airport.
(2) I've lost my pen. Can you help me to....it?
(3) He's a good friend of mine. I've....him for many years.
(4) Do you think they have forgotten that we were supposed to....here?
(5) During the year in which he worked in my office I....him very well.
(6) 'I didn't realise that the two of you had already....'
'Yes, we....each other very well.'
(7) They first....on holiday in Austria and....each other during the fortnight they spent there.
(8) Do you....her attractive?

G Composition

You and your wife/your husband/a friend (a) have invited some friends to dinner. Write a short dialogue about the reasons why they are already half an hour late (b) have gone to the airport to meet some friends. Write a short dialogue about what may have happened to them when their plane is already half an hour late.

PROGRESS TEST
How would you answer the following questions or statements, using forms of *may, might, can, can't* and *couldn't?*

(1) 'Perhaps they're sitting in a pub drinking.' (a) They ....They said they would have a drink before they met us. (b) They.... They're too nice to keep us waiting so long. (c) They....but perhaps they can't find the cinema. I think that's more likely.
(2) 'Perhaps their car has broken down.' (a) It....but I doubt it. (b) It.... It's very old. (c) It.... They've just had it repaired.
(3) 'Do you think it will rain tomorrow?' (a) The sky is cloudy. It....rain (b) The sky is clear but I suppose it....rain. (c) I don't think so, but it.... rain heavily at this time of year.
(4) 'I saw your brother in the street yesterday.' (a) You....He is abroad. (b) You....He goes past

your house on his way to work. (c) He lives in
another part of the town but he occasionally comes
here, so you....him.

13 The Railway Code

Two girls are travelling to work in London by train, as
they do every morning.

SUSAN   *We ought not to have got into a first-class carriage.* What
will happen if a ticket-collector comes? *We should*
5   *have thought of that.*
BRENDA We'll have to pay the difference in the fare, I
suppose. But the second-class carriages were all
full up. I had to stand all the way yesterday and
it's an hour's journey.
10   (The ticket collector comes into the compartment and
inspects the tickets)
TICKET COLLECTOR These are second-class season tickets.
You'll have to pay the full fare.
BRENDA You mean we must pay the difference.
15   TICKET COLLECTOR No, the full fare, I'm afraid.
BRENDA *You must be mistaken. That can't be true.*
TICKET COLLECTOR The rule is that if you buy an ordinary
second-class ticket and travel first class, you must
pay the difference, but if you have a second-class
20   season ticket, you must pay the whole fare. If
you don't believe me, you can take it up with the
stationmaster's office in London, but they'll tell
you the same thing.
BRENDA But that's unfair. *They must have been crazy to think*
25   *of a rule like that.* What will happen if I don't pay?
Do I have to get off?
TICKET COLLECTOR (patiently) You mustn't do that,
Miss. The train doesn't stop again before London.
But *you needn't pay me now.* I'll take down your

30   name and address and *you can pay the railway
              company later.*

BRENDA What would happen if I refused to pay then?

SUSAN   Brenda, you shouldn't be so awkward! It's no use
              taking it out on him. He doesn't make the rules.

35   TICKET COLLECTOR They would have to take you to court
              and you would have to pay a fine. Last year, a
              young lady refused to pay the fine, too, and in the
              end she had to go to prison.

BRENDA Do you think we should pay him, Susan?

40   SUSAN   Of course we should. We ought not to take up the
              poor man's time. He has all the other tickets to
              collect.

BRENDA All right. How much is it?

TICKET COLLECTOR Two pounds thirty pence.

45   BRENDA Heavens! *People who travel first-class every day must
              be well off.* Here you are. (giving him the money)
              You mustn't be angry. I know you have to do your job.

TICKET COLLECTOR That's all right, Miss. Plenty of people
              tell me what they think of the company. *But you*

50   *needn't have got in here,* in fact. *The second-class carriage
              at the front is empty.*

A   Comprehension

Which of the following statements is correct in the
context of the passage?

(1) The girls had (a) first-class tickets (b) second-class
season tickets (c) ordinary second-class tickets.

(2) The ticket collector said that the girls (a) had to
pay him the full fare immediately (b) had to get off
(c) could give him their names and addresses and
pay the railway company later.

(3) Susan (a) agreed that they shouldn't pay the full
fare (b) thought they ought to pay the railway
company later (c) thought they ought to pay the
ticket collector the full fare.

(4) Brenda (a) blamed the ticket collector for the argument (b) admitted that he had to do his duty (c)
thought he was mad.

(5) Brenda and Susan (a) didn't need to get into the first-class compartment (b) had to get into the first-class compartment (c) needn't have got into the first-class compartment because ....

B Words

Choose the word or phrase from the alternatives given which is closest in meaning to the words in italics in the context of the passage.

(1) *We should have thought of that* (1.4) (a) We had to think about that (b) We must have thought of that (c) We ought to have thought of that
(2) *Inspects* (1.11) (a) collects (b) counts (c) looks at
(3) *Think of* (1.24) (a) consider (b) invent (c) think about
(4) *You needn't pay me* (1.29) (a) you don't have to pay me (b) you mustn't pay me (c) you shouldn't pay me
(5) *Refused* (1.37) (a) said that she hadn't (b) said that she wouldn't (c) denied
(6) *Poor* (1.41) (a) unhappy (b) short of money (c) deserving sympathy
(7) *Well off* (1.46) (a) better somewhere else (b) rich (c) in good health
(8) *Tell me what they think of the company* (1.49) (a) say that they consider the company (b) tell me about the company (c) tell me their opinion of the company

C Patterns

(1a) *Mustn't* expresses prohibition or sometimes (*you mustn't*) suggests 'please don't' – *You mustn't be angry. I know you have to do your job.* Use it to complete these sentences.
    (a) You.... drive on the right-hand side of the road in England.
    (b) You.... travel by train without a ticket.
    (c) I.... run because I have a weak heart.

(1b) *Needn't* expresses absence of obligation (also expressed by *don't have to* and *don't need to*). *You needn't pay me now. You can pay the railway company later.* Use it to complete these sentences.

(a) You....do the whole exercise now. You can finish it at home.

(b) You....write to him. He already knows the news.

(c) You....wait for me. I'll meet you later.

(2a) The past forms of must·and needn't are *had to* and *didn't need to*. Use the correct one to complete these sentences.

(a) The second-class carriages were all full up. I.... stand all the way.

(b) A young lady refused to pay the fine so she.... go to prison.

(c) There were plenty of seats so I....stand.

(2b) There is an alternative past form to *didn't need to* – *needn't have* (+past participle). This is used when the action was done unnecessarily. *You needn't have got in here. The second-class carriage at the front is empty.* (But in fact the girls got in, because they did not realise this). Taking this into account, complete the following sentences with the correct form.

(a) As I had enough money for the fare, Susan.... (lend) me any.

(b) You.... (do) the washing-up alone. I would have helped you if you had asked me.

(c) She....(go) to prison. She could have paid the fine. I wonder why she didn't.

(3) *Must* and *will have to* are both used in the future to express obligation. Use each in turn to complete the following sentences.

(a) These are second-class season tickets. You.... pay the full fare.

(b) If you don't pay the fine, you.... go to prison.

(c) I....take down your name and address. That is the rule.

(4) *Ought to* and *should* are used to express an obligation (sometimes moral) which is not as strong as *must* or *have to*. The part forms are *ought to have* and *should have*,

in each case followed by the past participle. *We ought not to have got into a first-class carriage* (this automatically means that they got in); *we should have thought of that* (this automatically means that they didn't think of it). Put these sentences into the past, using each form in turn.

(a) You ought to write to your parents, John. Why don't you?

(b) You shouldn't be so awkward, Brenda. He might get angry.

(c) We ought not to take up the poor man's time. He has so much work to do.

(5a) *Must* is used in a different way from the patterns above to express logical probability:
People who travel first class every day must be well off
The past form of *must* with this meaning is *must have* +past participle:
They must have been crazy to think of a rule like that
Put the following sentences into the past.

(a) He speaks English perfectly. He must be English.

(b) She must be his sister. She looks just like him.

(c) She must be very attractive. All the men run after her.

(5b) The negative form of *must* with this meaning is expressed by *can't*:
You must be mistaken. That can't be true
Disagree with the following statements for the reasons given in brackets.

(a) It must be nine o'clock by now. It.... (not dark yet)

(b) He must be at home. The lights are on. He.... (left five minutes ago)

(c) She looks just like him. She must be his sister. She.... (only child)

(5c) The negative of *must have*+participle is expressed by *can't have* +participle (Present Perfect) or *couldn't have*+participle (Past). Disagree with the following statements for the reason given in brackets.

(a) I suppose she has lost her way. She.... (She has a map)

(b) I suppose he has spent all his money. He....
(I lent him £100 yesterday)

(c) I suppose you sent the letter to the wrong address. I.... (I remember writing the address down)

D Nouns and Articles

Some nouns are used without 'the' in certain cases when we are speaking of something in general terms but we use 'the' with them when we are thinking of a particular case. Compare the following:

She refused to pay the fine and had to go to prison

Poor woman! Her husband is in prison. She is going to the prison now to visit him

Supply the correct preposition and 'the' (where you think it is necessary) in the following sentences.

(1) If you refused to pay the fare, the railway company would take you....court.

(2) Thank heavens the children have gone back.... school.

(3) He's very ill. They'll have to take him....hospital.

(4) It's ten o'clock and she's still....bed.

(5) He's....hospital, having an operation. I'm going ....hospital to see him on Sunday.

(6) She went....school to see the headmaster about her son's progress.

(7) I'm going....harbour to meet my son. His ship's ....dock after six months ....sea.

(8) He never goes....church.

(9) They travel....office....train every morning. It's much too far to go ... foot.

(10) My husband's gone....work, the children are.... school and I'm....home cooking the dinner.

E Think Of and Think About

Complete the sentence with the correct preposition and then suggest another verb or phrase which means the same thing as *think of* or *think about* in each case.

(1) They must have been crazy to think....a rule like that.
(2) What do you think....the service on this line?
(3) Where are you thinking....going for your holidays this year?
(4) I've forgotten his name. I'll think....it in a minute.
(5) Are you going to buy a new car? I'm not sure. I'm still thinking....it.

F Phrasal Verbs – Take

Complete the sentences with one of the following prepositions – *after, back, down, in* (2), *off, on, out on, over, up* (3).

(1) If you don't believe me, you can take the matter.... with the railway company.
(2) I'll take....your name and address and you can pay the railway company later.
(3) It's no use taking it....the ticket collector. He doesn't make the rules.
(4) We ought not to take....the poor man's time. He's busy.
(5) You can see from his nose that he takes....his father.
(6) The plane is just going to take.... ·
(7) He's far too busy to take....any more work.
(8) The company have been taken....by a larger firm.
(9) If you speak slowly and clearly the students will take ... the meaning.
(10) I'm going to take....golf next year.
(11) When I visited Farley again, it took me....to my childhood.
(12) I'm afraid you've been taken....This pound note is not genuine.

G Composition

(1) You are travelling on the underground and when the the ticket collector comes, you discover that you have lost your ticket. Write a brief dialogue.

(2) You have parked your car outside a public building with a 'no parking' sign. A policeman sees it. Write a dialogue.

PROGRESS TEST

Choose the correct alternative in each case.

JUDGE Why did you refuse / deny to pay the fare?

MISS FITT The ticket collector said I must have paid / had to pay the full fare.

I didn't mind paying / to pay the difference.

JUDGE But I have already / yet explained that this is the company's rule. If you travel by the train / train you need / must accept these conditions.

MISS FITT The company must have been / had to be mad to think about / of a rule like / as that. They ought to / must charge the difference. After all, I needn't have bought / didn't need to buy a season ticket but I bought one.

JUDGE If you refuse / deny to pay you will / should have to go to the prison / prison. You mustn't / needn't go, of course, if you pay.

MISS FITT This mustn't / can't be true. The rule should / need be changed.

JUDGE I ought to / have to do my job.

MISS FITT All right, I'll pay. I don't want to go to the prison / prison.

JUDGE What a pity you didn't say that at the beginning!

There $\begin{matrix} \text{have to} \\ \text{must} \end{matrix}$ be more important things to discuss here.

14 The Case of the Mint and the Stamps

Inspector Watts has just arrived at Mr. Gosling's house to carry out an investigation into a burglary. The two men are in the dining room, where there is a large glass case full of gold and silver cups and beside it a wall safe, which
5 is open and empty.

WATTS Now, sir, what was stolen?

GOSLING Everything in the safe. About three hundred pounds in notes, some premium bonds and most important, my stamp collection, which
10 must be worth at least ten thousand pounds.

WATTS How do you think the thief got into the house?

GOSLING Through these french windows over here, which give on to the garden. He must have forced them open.

15 WATTS When did you discover the theft?

GOSLING This morning.

WATTS And what time did you go to bed last night?

GOSLING About eleven o'clock. Everything was in place so the thief must have got in during the night,
20 mustn't he?

WATTS How far away is your bedroom?

GOSLING My bedroom's upstairs on the other side of the house and I'm alone here at the moment. My wife and children are away on holiday. I didn't
25 hear anything. What surprises me is that the thief stole everything in the safe but left my cups. They're valuable, too.

WATTS   They're more difficult to dispose of, sir, and easier to trace. Now that I think of it, your photo-
30   graph was in the paper last week, wasn't it?

GOSLING   Yes, it was. I'd just won the County Golf Cup.

WATTS   Where was the photograph taken?

GOSLING   In this room. I was standing in front of the glass case, holding the cup.

35   WATTS   Whose idea was it to take the picture here?

GOSLING   Mine. I thought it was the most appropriate place.

WATTS   No doubt. But it may prove expensive.

GOSLING   Good heavens! Why?

40   WATTS   Because I expect the thief saw the same photo-graph as I did, with your wall safe next to the glass case. If I remember rightly, the article about you mentioned your stamp collection, didn't it?

45   GOSLING   Yes, it did.

WATTS   One more question, sir. Do you ever suck mints?

GOSLING   Are you serious, Inspector? You're not giving up the case already, are you? (angrily) No, I never eat mints.

50   WATTS   Then how did this get here? (He picks up a sweet wrapping from the floor.) May I use your 'phone, Mr. Gosling?

GOSLING   Certainly. Carry on, Inspector.

WATTS   Hello. Inspector Simmons, please. How long
55   has Minty Miller been inside, John? We sent him up three years ago? Find out when he was due to come out and ring me back, will you?

GOSLING   Who is Minty Miller?

WATTS   A professional safe-cracker, sir. He always sucks
60   mints to help his concentration, he once told me.

GOSLING   Good heavens! You must know him well. How often have you arrested him?

WATTS   Four or five times, always for the same thing.

GOSLING   What is he like?

65   WATTS   A quiet little man, but he used to be more care-ful. It was no use looking for fingerprints. But fancy him leaving the mint paper on the floor! That's what gave him away. (The telephone

rings.) I see. He came out of prison last Thurs-
70   day. Thanks, John.
GOSLING   That seems to settle the matter, doesn't it?
WATTS   Yes, sir, though I can't promise I'll get all your
          stamps back. So the next time you have your
          photograph taken, you won't tell everyone
75   where your safe is, will you?

A   Comprehension

Which of the following statements is correct in the context
of the passage?

(1) Mr Gosling's stamp collection (a) cost £10,000 (b)
    has been valued at £10,000 (c) is probably worth
    over £10,000.
(2) Mr Gosling did not hear the thief get into the house
    because (a) his bedroom is a long way away (b) the
    thief did not take the cups (c) he was alone in the
    house.
(3) The thief did not take the cups because (a) they
    were worthless (b) he was afraid of making a noise
    (c) they would have been hard for him to sell.
(4) Inspector Watts thinks (a) the photograph of Mr
    Gosling in the newspaper must have cost a lot of
    money (b) Mr Gosling should not have been
    photographed holding the cup (c) Mr Gosling
    should not have been photographed standing next
    to his safe.
(5) Inspector Watts (a) was only looking for sweet
    wrappings (b) did not expect to find fingerprints
    (c) forgot to look for fingerprints.

B   Words

Choose the word or phrase from the alternatives given
which is closest in meaning to the words in italics in the
context of the passage.

(1) *Stolen* (1.6) (a) robbed (b) taken (c) brought
(2) *During* (1.19) (a) for (b) at some time in (c) since
(3) *Alone* (1.23) (a) lonely (b) single (c) on my own

(4) *Think of* (1.29) (a) invent (b) remember (c) express my opinion about

(5) *Appropriate* (1.36) (a) suitable (b) convenient (c) private

(6) *May I* (1.51) (a) can I (b) should I (c) must I

(7) *Due to* (1.57) (a) expected to (b) obliged to (c) told to

(8) *You must know him well* (1.61) (a) I suppose you are a friend of his (b) It is your duty to meet him (c) You must have met him many times

(9) *What is he like?* (1.64) (a) How is he? (b) What kind of man is he? (c) What is he?

(10) *It was no use* (1.66) (a) I used not to (b) I don't usually (c) there was no point in.

C   Question Words

Answer the following questions about the passage and about yourself. Write complete sentences.

(1) *How* (a) did the thief get into the house? (b) did the Inspector find out that Minty Miller was no longer in prison? (c) do you come to the Institute/your school?

(2) *Who* (a) called Inspector Watts to his house? (b) robbed Mr Gosling? (c) is your teacher?

(3) *Who* (a) did Inspector Watts telephone? (b) had Inspector Watts arrested several times? (c) are you sitting next to?

(4) *Whose* (a) photograph appeared in the newspaper? (b) idea was it to take the photograph in the dining room? (c) sweet wrapping did the Inspector find?

(5) *What time* (a) did Mr Gosling go to bed? (b) do you get up on Sunday mornings? (c) do you have dinner?

(6) *Why* (a) did Inspector Watts think that taking the photograph in the dining room might prove expensive? (b) did he telephone Inspector Simmons? (c) are you studying English?

(7) *What is* (a) Minty Miller (b) your teacher (c) your ideal wife/husband *like?*

(8) *How long* (a) was Minty Miller in prison? (b) have

you been in this building? (c) have you been studying English?

(9) *How often* (a) has Inspector Watts arrested Minty
Miller? (b) do you have English classes? (c) do you
have lunch?

(10) *How far* (a) was Mr Gosling's bedroom from the
dining room? (b) is it from your house to the Insti-
tute/where you are living to your school? (c) is it
from here to New York?

D Question Tags

The most common use of question tags is in questions
which expect confirmation of the speaker's statement.
If the statement is affirmative, the tag is negative and
vice versa: – *Your photograph was in the paper last week, wasn't it?*
*You won't tell everyone where your safe is, will you? That seems
to settle the matter, doesn't it?* Complete the following sentences with the correct question tag.

(1) He's a nice man, ... ?
(2) You won't tell him about it, ... ?
(3) They haven't come back yet, ... ?
(4) You were in the house, ... ?
(5) He likes apples, ... ?
(6) The article mentioned your stamp collection, ... ?
(7) The thief must have got in during the night, ... ?
(8) He ought to be more careful, ... ?
(9) You don't believe that, ... ?
(10) He couldn't have done that, ... ?

E Phrasal Verbs – Carry

Complete the sentences with one of the following prepositions – *off, on* (2), *out, through*

(1) Inspector Watts is carrying .... an investigation
into a burglary.
(2) Carry .... with your work.
(3) He carries .... as if he were the boss.

(4) The actor forgot his lines but carried it .... so well that no one noticed.

(5) He carried the project .... in spite of the difficulties.

F Phrasal Verbs – Give

Complete the sentences with one of the following prepositions – *away, off, on to, out, up* (2)

(1) The french windows give....the garden.
(2) I wish I could give....smoking.
(3) The sweet wrapping gave Minty Miller ....
(4) I'm not going to give .... while I have a chance of winning.
(5) He tried to climb the mountain alone, but his strength gave .... and he had to be rescued.
(6) When I opened the bottle, it gave....a strong smell.

G Composition

(1) You arrive home and find that your house has been burgled. Write a brief dialogue between yourself and a policeman who has come to investigate.

(2) You have lost your dog. Write a brief dialogue between yourself and a policeman when you report that the dog is missing.

PROGRESS TEST
The following sentences are answers to questions. The part in italic type is the real answer. Ask the questions.

(1) The thief got in *through the french windows.*
(2) Birmingham is *110 miles* from London.
(3) The thief didn't take the cups *because they would have been difficult to dispose of.*
(4) The photograph was taken *in the dining room.*
(5) It was *Mr Gosling's* idea to have the photograph taken there.
(6) Minty Miller was in prison *for three years.*
(7) I am *very well.*

(8) He is *a quiet little man.*
(9) He is *a teacher.*
(10) *Inspector Watts* telephoned Inspector Simmons
(11) Inspector Watts telephoned *Inspector Simmons.*
(12) I attend classes *three times a week.*

15 About 28 g of Common Sense

One day early in 1971 Britain changed to decimal
currency. *The Government introduced a new monetary system*
and new coins at the same time. *It was fairly easy for the*
young to accept the system because *they had learnt mathematics*
5   *not long before* but *it was* hard for the old, who had spent
all their lives buying and selling in pounds, shillings and
pence, and *especially hard for the blind,* who had to learn to
recognise the value of the new coins by touch alone. There
were angry arguments in shops in the first few days after
10   decimalisation and some customers could not work out
their bills and offered shopkeepers a handful of coins,
trusting that they would not be cheated. But the change
to decimal currency was a fairly simple operation compared to what will happen when Britain adopts the SI*
15   system of weights and measures.
    Change always provokes opposition and it is said that
the opposition to metrication in Britain is due to sentiment
and isolationism. It is true that our weights and measures
are part of our language. There are hundreds of expressions
20   that would sound ridiculous to an Englishman if they were
metricated: –'A miss is as good as a mile'; 'he came down
on me like a ton of bricks'; 'he wants his pound of flesh'.
Many English people believe that *life will* somehow *be*
different when they have to buy butter by the kilo, not by the pound,
25   and milk by the litre instead of by the pint.
    Even *the traditional English summer game, cricket,* will be

SI* — Systeme International d'Unités

D

affected. The length of a cricket pitch will not be 22 yards any more but 20.1168 metres. For cricketers, this will be almost as difficult to accept and remember as it was for
30 people a few hundred years ago to accept that *the Earth goes round the Sun.*

But there are also very practical reasons for keeping the present system. One is that the change will be very expensive. So many machines will have to be altered or
35 replaced that economists have worked out that the money spent would be enough to build 400 hospitals. Another reason is that although the case for SI mainly depends on the advantages for British industry in selling goods to Europe, Britain's biggest customer abroad, the
40 United States, is not going to give up the old units and even on the Continent people still prefer the metric system, which is somewhat different. There is no point in changing unless everyone else does the same thing.

Government officials are busy working on schemes for
45 educating the public but they are finding it difficult to work up enthusiasm for SI. The British are famous for their respect for tradition but also renowned for their common sense. Perhaps the latter has more to do with their distrust of SI than the former.

A Comprehension

Which of the following statements is correct in the context of the passage?

(1) It was difficult for the blind to get used to decimal currency because (a) they were old (b) they had forgotten the mathematics they had learnt at school (c) the new coins were of different shape and size from the old ones.

(2) In the first few days after decimalisation some customers (a) refused to pay their bills (b) tried to cheat shopkeepers (c) let shopkeepers take the right amount of money from their hands

(3) One of the main arguments against adopting SI units in Britain is that (a) they will alter the English

language (b) they will make it impossible to play cricket (c) the change will cost more money than it is worth

(4) SI units are at present used (a) in some European countries (b) all over the world (c) in the United States

(5) The author thinks that the opposition to SI in Britain is due to the British people's (a) respect for tradition (b) suspicion of anything new (c) common sense

B Words

Choose the word or phrase from the alternatives given which is closest in meaning to the words in italics in the context of the passage.

(1) *The young* (1.4) (a) young people (b) children (c) youths
(2) *Work out* (1.10) (a) calculate (b) estimate (c) pay
(3) *Somehow* (1.23) (a) in some way (b) for some reason (c) anyway
(4) *Renowned* (1.47) (a) famous (b) infamous (c) notorious
(5) *The latter* (1.48) (a) the previous word (b) tradition (c) common sense

C Patterns

Study the pattern in italic type in each case and then reproduce it, substituting the words given but taking care to form the verbs correctly. Change or put in articles, possessives, prepositions where necessary.

(1) *The Government introduced a new monetary system. It was fairly easy for the young to accept the system*
    (a) The company/accounting method/quite simple/ staff/get used to/method
    (b) The Government/tax system/rather hard/rich/ accept/system

    (c) The headmaster/teaching method/rather difficult/teachers/adopt/method

(2) *The new system was especially hard for the blind*
    (a) tax/particularly harsh on/rich
    (b) discotheque/extremely popular with/young
    (c) allowances/fairly generous to/unemployed

(3) *The Earth goes round the Sun*
    (a) Moon/go round/Earth
    (b) present/be different from/past
    (c) sun/rise in/east

(4) *Life will be different when they have to buy butter by the kilo, not by the pound*
    (a) petrol/litre/gallon
    (b) milk/litre/pint
    (c) cloth/metre/yard

(5) *They had learnt mathematics not long before*
    (a) They/study/physics/some years before
    (b) She/learn/English/at school
    (c) He/practise/medicine/as a young man

(6) *Cricket is the traditional English summer game*
    (a) Football/English/winter
    (b) Baseball/American/summer
    (c) Golf/Scottish/summer

D Use of the Definite Article with Abstract Nouns

Study the following sentences and then complete the sentences in the exercise by writing the definite article, *the,* only where it is necessary, in the spaces. It will not be necessary when we are using an abstract noun in general terms, when it is only qualified by an adjective in front of it, or when the qualifying words after it only refer to place.

Life is sometimes difficult
Modern life is often complicated
He has written a book on life in fifth-century Athens
He has written a book on the life of the ancient Greeks
He decided to give up the life he had been leading

(1) I am fond of. . . . music.
(2) I prefer. . . . classical music.
(3) My father loves. . . . music of the eighteenth century.
(4) The children liked. . . . music we heard on the radio last night.
(5) . . . . opposition to. . . . metrication in Britain is due to. . . . sentiment and. . . . isolationism.
(6) The British are famous for their respect for. . . . tradition but also renowned for. . . . common sense.
(7) The Government are finding it difficult to work up . . . .enthusiasm for. . . .SI system of weights and measures.
(8) . . . . exploration of. . . . outer space has aroused. . . . curiosity all over the world.

E It and There

It is used as an impersonal subject when the subject would otherwise be long and complicated, and in passive constructions. Use the patterns in the following sentences, putting the verb *be* in the most appropriate tense and form.

(1) *It was easy for the young to accept the new system*
   (a) difficult/old/get used to/currency
   (b) hard/English/get used to/weights and measures
   (c) impossible/poor/pay/taxes

(2) *It is true that our weights and measures are complicated*
   (a) clear/the public/suspicious
   (b) obvious/the Government/convinced
   (c) understandable/the workers/conservative

(3) *It is said that the opposition to metrication is due to sentiment*
   (a) believe/the accident/fog
   (b) think/the air crash/sabotage
   (c) report/delay/bad weather conditions

There is used impersonally as subject to show the existence of something. *There are hundreds of expressions* means 'hundreds of expressions exist'. Use the patterns in the following sentences, as above.

(4) *There are practical reasons for keeping the old system*
   (a) good arguments/rejecting SI

(b) excellent opportunities here/investing money
(c) interesting proposals/improving the law

(5) *There is no point in changing unless everyone else does the same thing*
(a) value/in protesting/other people/think the same way
(b) hope/of persuading them/the majority of people/ have the same idea
(c) possibility/of preventing it/a lot of people/put forward the same objections

F   Phrasal Verbs – Work

Complete the sentences with one of the following pre-positions – *off, on, out* (2), *up*

(1) Economists have worked....that the money spent would be enough to build 400 hospitals.
(2) Government officials are working....schemes for educating the public.
(3) They are finding it difficult to work....enthusiasm for SI.
(4) Let the child run about. He has so much energy that he has to work it....somehow
(5) There was trouble at first but eventually everything worked....according to plan.

G   Composition

(1) Explain what happened in Britain when the Government introduced decimal currency.
(2) There are various reasons why the public in Britain do not like SI. What are they?
(3) Explain how the tax system is organised in your country.

PROGRESS TEST
Choose the correct alternative in each case.

The British $\begin{matrix} \text{are} \\ \text{is} \end{matrix}$ famous for $\begin{matrix} \text{their} \\ \text{its} \end{matrix}$ respect for $\begin{matrix} \text{the tradition.} \\ \text{tradition.} \end{matrix}$

$\begin{matrix} \text{The visitors} \\ \text{Visitors} \end{matrix}$ come from other countries to see ceremonies

like the changing
as changing of the guard, which takes place in

London and attracts the youngs and the olds. Once
the young the old.

the American lady wanted to photograph one soldier who
an a

was outside the Buckingham Palace. There was hot and the
Buckingham Palace. It a

soldier was tired after several hours in the sun. Sometimes
a

soldiers lose the patience with tourists. When the lady
patience a

told him to stand still he trod on the foot. There was a
her It

report in one of the newspapers but the soldier's command-
ing officer was the expert in the diplomacy. He explained
an diplomacy.

that the soldier had been suffering from the sunstroke and
a sunstroke

invited the lady to watch the Duke of Edinburgh play
a a

the polo.
polo.

16 Good and Bad Monsters

A lot of people believe that television has a harmful effect
on children. *A few years ago, the same criticisms were made of the
cinema.* But although *child psychologists have spent a great deal of
time studying this problem*, there is not much evidence that
5   television brings about juvenile delinquency.
   *Few people in the modern world share the views of parents a
hundred years ago. In those days, writers for children carefully
avoided any reference to sex in their books* but *had no inhibitions*

about including scenes of violence. These days children are often
10 brought up to think freely about sex but violence is
discouraged. Nevertheless, *television companies receive a*
large number of letters every week complaining about programmes with adult themes being shown at times when a
few young children may be awake. *Strangely enough,* the
15 *parents* who complain about these programmes *see no harm*
in cartoon films for children in which the villain, usually either
an animal or a monster, but in some cases a human being,
suffers one brutal punishment after another.

The fact is that, as every parent knows, different things
20 frighten different children. *One child can read a ghost story*
without having bad dreams while another cannot bear to have the
book in his bedroom. In the same way, *there is little consistency*
about the things that terrify adults. Almost every one has an irrational
private fear but *while some of us cannot stand the sight of spiders,*
25 for example, *others are frightened of snakes or rats.*

The evidence collected suggests, however, that neither
the subject nor the action in itself frightens children. The
context in which cruelty or violence occurs is much more
important.
30 A good guide to what is psychologically healthy for a
small child is therefore provided by a television series in
which a boy and girl are supposed to be exploring distant
planets with their parents. *In each story, they* encounter
strange monsters and *find themselves in dangerous situations*
35 but the parents are reassuring and sensible, as a child's
parents should be in real life. There is an adult character
who is a coward and a liar, but both the children are brave
and of course every story ends happily.

Some people think children should be exposed to the
40 problems of real life as soon as possible, but they cannot
help seeing these through news programmes. When they
are being entertained, the healthiest atmosphere is one in
which the hero and heroine are *children like themselves who*
behave naturally and confidently in any situation.

A Comprehension

Which of the following statements is correct in the context
of the passage?

(1) Psychologists (a) believe that television causes juvenile delinquency (b) think that television programmes are harmless (c) cannot find much evidence of a direct connection between television and juvenile delinquency.

(2) Parents who write letters of complaint to television companies (a) do not like adult programmes (b) are afraid their children will be harmed by seeing adult programmes (c) think cartoon films are too violent.

(3) (a) Children who read ghost stories have bad dreams (b) Almost everyone is secretly afraid of something (c) All adults are afraid of spiders.

(4) The television programmes that frighten children are those that (a) include scenes of violence (b) deal with unpleasant subjects (c) contain cruelty or violence in a context they associate with their own situation.

(5) The television series mentioned is healthy because (a) the children are shown as brave and confident (b) it is unreal (c) the only bad character is adult.

B Words

Choose the word or phrase from the alternatives given which is closest in meaning to the words in italics in the context of the passage.

(1) *a great deal of* (1.3) (a) a large number of (b) a lot of (c) many.

(2) *few* (1.6) (a) not many (b) little (c) some.

(3) *share* (1.6) (a) agree with (b) have a part of (c) belong to.

(4) *had no inhibitions about* (1.8) (a) were not prevented from (b) were not stopped from (c) were not worried about.

(5) *a large number of* (1.12) (a) a lot of (b) a considerable amount of (c) a few.

(6) *the fact is* (1.19) (a) this is true (b) what matters is (c) the truth of the matter is.

(7) *as every parent knows* (1.19) (a) like each parent believes (b) as all parents know (c) as all fathers know.

(8) *cannot stand the sight of* (1.24) (a) do not like the look of (b) cannot bear to look at (c) are afraid of the view of.

(9) *sensible* (1.35) (a) having refined feelings (b) having common sense (c) understanding.

(10) *cannot help* (1.40) (a) are unable to assist in (b) are incapable of assisting in (c) are unable to avoid.

C Patterns

(1) *A lot of* can be used with countable or uncountable nouns but *a large number of* is only found with countables – *television companies receive a large number of letters every week* – and *a great deal of* is only found with uncountables – *child psychologists have spent a great deal of time studying this problem.* In general, we prefer these forms to *many* and *much* respectively in affirmative sentences, but in negative sentences we would usually say 'television companies don't receive many letters' or 'psychologists haven't spent much time on this problem'.

Change the sentences below, replacing *a lot of* with the correct alternative form and then put them all in the negative.

(a) He earns a lot of money in his new job.

(b) There were a lot of people at the wedding.

(c) He has done a lot of work this year.

(d) She has a lot of friends.

(e) A lot of people believe that television has a harmful effect on children.

(2) *Few* means 'not many' and *little* means 'not much' – *Few people in the modern world share the views of parents a hundred years ago* – *There is little consistency about the things that terrify adults.* But *a few* means 'some but not many', or 'not many, but enough'. *A little* means 'some, but not much'. – *A few years ago, the same criticisms were made of the cinema!*

Substitute the correct alternative form in the following sentences for the words in italic type.

(a) He has *not much* time for study.

(b) There are *not many* players who can beat him.

(c) I have *some* photographs at home that might interest you.

(d) His aunt left him *some* money when she died, which is enough for him to live on.

(e) I have brought you *some* flowers for your birthday.

(f) There is *not much* point in arguing with her.

(g) *Not many* television programmes are as popular as this one.

(h) I need *some* help. Will you hold this ladder, please?

(i) He has *not many* friends.

(j) Come here! I want to give you *some* advice.

(3) *No* and *not any* are commonly used as negatives of *some*. *Not any* is more frequently found in spoken English. They are used with countables and uncountables – *In those days, writers for children had no inhibitions about including scenes of violence* – *Strangely enough* (these) *parents see no harm in cartoon films for children.*

Change the *no* form to *not any* in the following sentences.

(a) He has *no* money.

(b) It will do him *no* harm.

(c) I have *no* complaints.

(d) There are *no* simple answers to the problem.

(e) I have *no* hope of winning the match.

(4) *One* and *another* are used in singular comparisons, *some* and *others* in plural comparisons:

One child can read a ghost story without having bad dreams while another cannot bear to have the book in his bedroom

While some of us cannot stand the sight of spiders, others are frightened of snakes or rats.

Change the following sentences to the plural form. Remember to change the verb forms where necessary.

(a) One man enjoys games while another finds them boring.

(b) One family spends every night looking at television while another never turns it on.

(c) One person is terrified of spiders while another cannot stand rats.

(d) One boss dictates his letters straightaway while another prefers to write them out first.

(e) One girl covers her face with make-up while another never uses it.

(5) *Any* can mean 'it doesn't matter which' or 'of whatever kind', apart from its use in (3) (above):
Children like themselves who behave naturally and confidently in any situation
Writers for children carefully avoided any reference to sex in their books
Substitute *any* for the phrases in italics in the following sentences:

(a) He is so fond of television that he looks at *a* programme of *whatever kind* that is on.

(b) You can take *it doesn't matter which* train – they all stop at London Bridge.

(c) *A* programme *of whatever kind* that includes unnecessary violence may be bad for children.

(d) You can ask me *a* question *of whatever kind* you like.

(e) He is such a good actor that he can play *a* part *of whatever kind*.

(6) It is possible to write *all the people* and *all the things* in English but when we speak in general terms we prefer *everyone* (*everybody*) or *everything*.
These words are all used with a singular verb:
Almost everyone has an irrational private fear
Use them to make better sentences, replacing the words in italic type and changing the verb forms where necessary.

(a) *All the people* want peace.

(b) Please help me. I can't carry *all the things*.

(c) He's very popular. *All the people* like him.

(d) A few years ago almost *all the people* went to the cinema every week.

(e) *All the things* come to those who wait.

(7) *Each* and *every* (both singular) can sometimes be used interchangeably:
Television companies still receive a large number of letters every (*each*) *week*. But *each* usually draws attention to an individual member or part of a group or considers them one by one, instead of all together:

In each story, they find themselves in dangerous situations
Substitute *each* and *every* for the words in italic type
in the following sentences and change plural forms
where necessary.
(a) *All the programmes* are checked to make sure that
they are suitable for children.
(b) *All the students* were given forms to fill in.
(c) *All the countries* have their own systems of education.
(d) *All the firms* have agreed to send representatives
to the conference.
(e) *All the teachers* will be responsible for their own
students.

D Phrasal Verbs – Bring

Complete the sentences with one of the following prepositions – *about, on, out* (2), *round* (2), *up* (2).
(1) There is not much evidence that television brings
    ....juvenile delinquency.
(2) These days children are often brought....to think
    freely about sex.
(3) The publishers are bringing....his new book at
    Christmas.
(4) It took a long time to bring people....to the idea
    that violence can be a worse influence on children
    than sex.
(5) At the last meeting of the Town Council, he brought
    ....the subject of juvenile delinquency.
(6) His study of child psychology brought....the fact
    that different children are afraid of different things.
(7) The girl has fainted. Throw some water on her face
    to bring her....
(8) He was caught in the rain last night. That may have
    brought.... his cold.

E Composition

Briefly describe (a) a popular television programme for
children in your country (b) what happens in the Euro-
vision song contest or a similar competition.

PROGRESS TEST

Choose the correct alternative in each case.

$\dfrac{\text{These}}{\text{Those}}$ days I don't watch television but $\dfrac{\text{a few}}{\text{few}}$ years ago

I used to watch it $\dfrac{\text{all the nights.}}{\text{every night.}}$ I was often $\dfrac{\text{little}}{\text{a little}}$ tired

in the evenings and there are $\dfrac{\text{a few}}{\text{few}}$ forms of entertainment

that demand as $\dfrac{\text{few}}{\text{little}}$ effort as television. Unfortunately,

there are $\dfrac{\text{a great deal of}}{\text{a large number of}}$ people in my family; $\dfrac{\text{some}}{\text{any}}$

wanted to see $\dfrac{\text{a}}{\text{one}}$ programme while $\dfrac{\text{others}}{\text{the other}}$ preferred

$\dfrac{\text{another.}}{\text{other.}}$ I was happy to look at $\dfrac{\text{some}}{\text{any}}$ programme but

$\dfrac{\text{the others}}{\text{another}}$ spent $\dfrac{\text{a large number of}}{\text{a great deal of}}$ time arguing $\dfrac{\text{each night}}{\text{all the nights}}$

and there was $\dfrac{\text{no}}{\text{any}}$ way of settling the matter except by

selling the set. Now $\dfrac{\text{everyone}}{\text{all the people}}$ at home $\dfrac{\text{read}}{\text{reads}}$ instead.

17 Your Business is My Business

Frank Hemsley is a young salesman attending a business conference in the north of England. He sits down at the bar of the hotel next to an older man.

5

FRANK   Hello. I hope you don't mind if I introduce myself. *I'm on my own here*, you see. My name's Hemsley.

TOWNSEND   Mine is Townsend. *I'm by myself, too.* Pleased to meet you.

FRANK   I represent Hunt and Platt. (He shows

10	Townsend the button he is wearing in the lapel of his jacket).
TOWNSEND	They've got a good name in the wool trade.
FRANK	To tell the truth, I haven't been there long, but I think *I've already caught the sales manager's*
15	*eye. I'm looking forward to promotion in two or three years' time.* I notice you're not wearing your conference button.
TOWNSEND	No. They make me feel conspicuous. (He sees another delegate passing and greets him).
20	Hello, Arthur.
FRANK	*Is he a friend of yours?*
TOWNSEND	Not exactly. We do a lot of business together.
FRANK	One of our representatives nearly lost his job yesterday because my boss saw him speaking
25	to that fellow. His name's Arthur Wakefield, isn't it, and he's the Sales Manager of Grossley Brothers. They're our biggest rivals.
TOWNSEND	I suppose they must be. But your boss's attitude seems rather extreme.
30 FRANK	He's frightened that someone will tell Grossleys our business secrets. That Wakefield is very cunning, they say. He was trying to buy this representative of ours a drink, so we can guess what his real idea was. He wanted to
35	find out about our machine.
TOWNSEND	Your glass is empty. What are you going to have?
FRANK	Very kind of you. A pint of bitter, please.
TOWNSEND	Mine's a light ale, barman. Now, you were
40	telling me about that new machine of yours.
FRANK	Oh, was I? But perhaps I shouldn't say any more. After all, you're one of Grossleys' customers.
TOWNSEND	But we could easily become yours, if we saw
45	some advantage in it.
FRANK	It's just that we've got a new machine from Japan that mixes natural and artificial fibres very economically so *our prices will be much lower than Grossleys'.*
50 TOWNSEND	*Your machine would be very interesting to a company*

like mine. The public can't always tell the difference in quality but they can always recognise a difference in price.

FRANK   Will you let me buy you the other half?

55   TOWNSEND   No, thank you. I must make a telephone call. It's been very nice meeting you.

FRANK   (on his own again) What a pleasant fellow! I wonder which company he represents. (He looks at his 'Guide to Delegates' and reads out

60   to himself, horrified). 'Townsend, R. G., Managing Director, Grossley Brothers Limited.

A   Comprehension

Which of the following statements is correct in the context of the passage?

(1) Mr Townsend isn't wearing his conference button because (a) he has lost it (b) he doesn't want Frank to know his name (c) he doesn't want to be recognised immediately

(2) Mr Townsend knows Arthur Wakefield well because (a) they work for the same company (b) Wakefield bought him a drink (c) he is a customer of Wakefield's

(3) Frank is not sure if he should tell Mr Townsend about the machine because he thinks Townsend (a) works for a rival firm (b) is a friend of Wakefield's (c) is one of Grossley Brothers' customers

(4) Mr Townsend persuades Frank to talk about the machine by (a) buying him a drink (b) promising not to tell Grossleys about it (c) suggesting that he may transfer his business from Grossleys to Frank's firm

(5) Mr Townsend probably goes to telephone (a) someone at Grossley Brothers (b) his wife (c) the hotel manager

B   Words

Choose the word or phrase from the alternatives given

which is closest in meaning to the words in italics in the context of the passage.

(1) *Attending* (1.1) (a) paying attention to (b) following (c) present at
(2) *Conference* (1.2) (a) lecture (b) reunion (c) meeting, with lectures
(3) *On my own* (1.5) (a) lonely (b) by myself (c) without help
(4) *To tell the truth* (1.13) (a) not to lie (b) to say honestly (c) to be honest with you
(5) *Price* (1.53) (a) value (b) worth (c) cost

C   Patterns

(1) *Your machine would be very interesting to a company like mine*
Study this pattern and then reproduce it, substituting the words given but changing the pronoun to the correct possessive form.

(a) He/knowledge/useful in a firm/we
(b) We/experience/valuable in a project/they
(c) I/investment/important to a country/you
(d) They/advice/helpful in a situation/she

(2) *Is he a friend of yours?*
Note form used here – *yours*, not 'your'. In the same way, we would say: *No, he's a friend of Arthur Wakefield's*. Use this pattern in the same way for question and answer, substituting the words given and changing pronouns and nouns to the correct possessive form.

(a) she/cousin/he? No, she/cousin/his wife
(b) he/colleague/you? No, he/colleague/my brother
(c) you/employee/we? No, I /employee/Mr Townsend
(d) we/customers/they? No, we/customers/Hunt and Platt

(3) *I've already caught the sales manager's eye*
Repeat the pattern, substituting the words given and changing to the correct possessive form.

(a) He/give away/the company/secret
(b) We/reply to/the customer/letter
(c) She/attract/the boss/attention

(4) *Our prices will be much lower than Grossleys'*
Repeat the pattern, as in (3).

    (a) Your garden/is prettier/your neighbours
    (b) Frank's attitude/is more naive/his rivals
    (c) My car/is faster/my parents

(5) *I'm looking forward to promotion in two or three years' time*
Use this form of the possessive in place of the words in italics in the following sentences, but notice that we say *in a year or two's time* (not 'in one or two years')

    (a) He always does a good *work of a day*
    (b) I'm going away for *a holiday of three weeks*
    (c) I'll see you again in *a time of two or three months*
    (d) He is hoping for promotion in *a time of a year or two*

D   On My Own and By Myself

(1) These are two different ways of expressing the idea: 'I am alone'. Use each in turn in place of the words italicised in the following sentences, changing the persons where appropriate.

    (a) If you'd rather be *alone*, I'll leave you.
    (b) He doesn't like drinking *alone*.
    (c) The children have gone to the cinema so we are *alone*.
    (d) Children usually prefer to play *alone*.

(2) *By . . . . self* is also used to mean 'without help'. *Johnny can tie his shoes by himself now.* Use this form in place of the words italicised, changing the persons where appropriate.

    (a) Can you manage to lift that case *without help?*
    (b) He is experienced enough to deal with clients *without help*.
    (c) The children are building a playhouse *without help*.
    (d) We won't need your help now. We've repaired it *without help*.

E   Noun Groups

Nouns are often used as if they were **adjectives** – '*Frank*

Hemsley is attending a business conference: I must make a telephone call.
Write down the correct group from these descriptions. Note that nouns used in this way are always singular – a lighter for lighting cigarettes is a *cigarette lighter*.

  (1) a dish made of rice
  (2) a frame of a window
  (3) a brush for painting
  (4) a heater for water
  (5) a race for motors
  (6) a word known in every household
  (7) the range of prices
  (8) a proprietor of newspapers
  (9) an attraction for tourists
(10) a dealer in (works of) art.
(11) a room for sitting (in)
(12) a dress for a party
(13) a collector of tickets
(14) a ticket for a season
(15) a case made of glass
(16) a safe in the wall
(17) a collection of stamps
(18) a game played in summer
(19) a story about ghosts
(20) a programme broadcasting the news

F   Say and Tell

Complete the sentences, using one of these verbs in the correct form.

  (1) He's frightened that someone will.... Grossleys our business secrets.
  (2) That Wakefield is very cunning, they....
  (3) You were.... me about that new machine of yours.
  (4) Perhaps I ought not to.... any more.
  (5) To.... the truth, I haven't been there long.
  (6) The little boy doesn't know how to.... the time yet.
  (7) She.... that she can't.... the difference between butter and margarine.

(8) I always....the children a story before they go to bed.

(9) I'll give you a discount on this order. Shall we....10 per cent?

(10) He should have found out who Townsend was before speaking to him. That goes without....

G Pronunciation (3)

In each group of four words below, three words rhyme but one does not. Choose the word that does not rhyme with the others in the group.

	(a)	(b)	(c)	(d)
(1)	wait	rate	great	beat
(2)	boys	noise	voice	toys
(3)	force	worse	horse	course
(4)	prove	love	above	glove
(5)	share	bear	fear	fare
(6)	young	tongue	sung	wrong
(7)	case	race	phrase	base
(8)	watch	catch	match	patch
(9)	pound	round	owned	drowned
(10)	due	through	who	though

H Composition

(1) You have left an article of clothing in a cloakroom at a restaurant and then lost the cloakroom ticket. Write a dialogue in which you try to make the cloakroom attendant give you back the article.

(2) Frank Hemsley's boss has seen him talking to Mr Townsend. Write a short dialogue between them.

(3) Mr Townsend tells Arthur Wakefield about his conversation with Frank Hemsley. Write the dialogue.

PROGRESS TEST

Frank Hemsley is a friend of me. / mine. His / Her office is next door

to mine / the mine at Hunt and Platt. Frank is independent.

He likes to work [on his own / himself] and is annoyed by any interference. 'The [companies / company's] policy is that [its / his] customers are [my / mine] and I have to solve the [customers' / customer] problems [by myself. / by themselves.] Unfortunately, some customers are friends of the [sales manager's / sales managers] and he is always asking them for [their / his] opinion of [my / mine] technique. [Grossleys / Grossleys'], representatives are better off. When I have two or three [years / years'] experience, I may change [my / the] job' 'I wouldn't like to be one of Arthur [Wakefields / Wakefield's] men,' I said. 'A cousin of [mine / me] used to work for him and he only got one [week / week's] holiday a year.'

18 Sometimes They Seem Almost Human

Dolphins have become a popular attraction at zoos in recent years. *They are more interesting than lions and tigers because they are livelier* and perform tricks, like circus animals. But although they are more willing to cooperate with the
5   trainer than other mammals in captivity, they get bored if they are asked to do the same trick twice. This is one reason for believing that they are very intelligent.
    Dolphins are regarded as the friendliest creatures in the sea and stories of them helping drowning sailors have been
10 common since Roman times. We now have more reliable evidence of their usefulness than sailors' tales. In South

Africa, two dolphins have been trained to help swimmers
in difficulties and drive sharks away from the beach.

The more we learn about dolphins, the more we realise
15 that they are better organised and their society is more
complex than people previously imagined. They look after
other dolphins when they are ill, care for pregnant mothers
and protect the weakest in the community, as we do.

Some scientists have suggested that dolphins have a
20 language but it is much more probable that they communicate with each other without needing 'words'. They
have an echo-location system which is similar to a bat's
and much more sensitive than our hearing, so the most
important task of a dolphin's brain is to transmit and
25 receive sound.

Whales, especially the smaller types, like the killer
whale, *are probably as intelligent as dolphins* and some
scientists claim that they are the most intelligent species
in the world, apart from man. *The great whales have the*
30 *same brain power as the smaller ones* but it is not so easy to
study them because they cannot be kept in captivity for
long and they live in the deeper, less accessible parts of
the ocean. Nevertheless, *the* only great *whale* kept in a zoo
for a year *learned as fast as a dolphin.*

35 Could any of these mammals be more intelligent than
man? The question cannot be answered because our aims
and interests are different from dolphins' and whales'.
They are better adapted to their environment *than we are and*
find food more easily. As a result, *they are much more attracted* by
40 pleasure for its own sake *than men and are not nearly so*
interested in dominating other species. Certainly *the most common*
argument in favour of man's superiority over them – we can kill
them more easily than they can kill us – *is the least satisfact-*
ory. On the contrary, the more we discover about these
45 remarkable creatures, the less we appear superior when we
destroy them.

A   Comprehension

Which of the following statements is correct in the context
of the passage?

(1) We realise that dolphins in zoos are very intelligent

because (a) they can perform tricks (b) they are bored by having to repeat the same trick (c) they are better-tempered than other animals.

(2) Dolphins (a) communicate with each other without using sounds (b) communicate with each other without using 'words' (c) have a language of their own.

(3) (a) Dolphins are undoubtedly the most intelligent species in the sea (b) The great whales are more intelligent than the smaller ones (c) killer whales are believed to be the most intelligent species in the world.

(4) We know less about the great whales than about dolphins because (a) we have never been able to keep one in captivity (b) they do not come to the surface of the ocean (c) it is harder to observe their habits.

(5) The argument that we can kill whales and dolphins more easily than they can kill us (a) proves that we are more intelligent than they are (b) proves that we are less intelligent than they are (c) does not prove anything with regard to intelligence.

B Words

Choose the word or phrase from the alternatives given which is closest in meaning to the words in italics in the context of the passage.

(1) *Popular* (1.1) (a) ordinary (b) common (c) liked by many people.
(2) *Livelier* (1.3) (a) more alive (b) more living (c) more active.
(3) *Perform* (1.3) (a) do (b) make (c) act.
(4) *Trained* (1.12) (a) taught (b) educated (c) learned.
(5) *More sensitive* (1.23) (a) more sensible (b) finer (c) more refined.
(6) *Task* (1.24) (a) work (b) hard work (c) job.
(7) *Like* (1.26) (a) as (b) such as (c) similar to.
(8) *Ones* (1.30) (a) whales (b) some (c) any.

(9) *Fast* (1.34) (a) quick (b) quickly (c) rapid.
(10) *On the contrary* (1.44) (a) on the other hand (b) in
    reverse (c) the opposite is true.

C Patterns

Study the pattern in italic type in each case and then
reproduce it, substituting the words given but taking care
to form the verbs correctly. Change or put in articles,
possessives, prepositions where necessary.

(1A) *Whales are probably as intelligent as dolphins*
   (a) He/already/tall/his father.
   (b) Cats/seldom/friendly/dogs.
   (c) Flats/almost/expensive/houses.

(1B) *The whale learned as fast as a dolphin*
   (a) Teachers work/hard/students.
   (b) I came/soon/I could.
   (c) He did/well/he expected.

(1C) *The great whales have the same brain power as the smaller
    ones*
   (a) She takes/size in shoes/I do.
   (b) Robert catches/train to work/his boss.
   (c) He asked/questions about the job/you did.

(2A) *They are more interesting than lions and tigers because they
    are livelier*
   (a) Joan/popular/Susan/she/pretty.
   (b) I/patient/my son/I/old.
   (c) The river/dangerous/the swimming pool/it/deep.

This comparison can be expressed in a different way –
'Lions and tigers are less interesting than dolphins because
they are not so lively'. Change the sentences you have
written in the same way, changing tenses if necessary.

(2B) *They are better adapted* (to their environment) *than we
    are and find food more easily*
   (a) Modern zoos/built/earlier ones/house animals/
       comfortably.
   (b) The new model/designed/the old machine/do
       job/efficiently.

(c) The article/written/the official report/put forward the argument/convincingly.

This comparison can also be expressed in a different way – 'We are not so well adapted to our environment as dolphins are and do not find food so easily'. Change the sentences you have written in the same way.

(3) *They are much more attracted* (by pleasure for its own sake) *than men and not nearly so interested in dominating other species*
   (a) Dolphins/inventive/other animals in captivity/willing to repeat the same tricks.
   (b) Cricket/complicated to understand/football/exciting to watch.
   (c) A ship's radar/reliable/a man's eyesight/dependent on weather conditions.

Now repeat the same sentences, substituting 'much less' for 'not nearly so' in each case.

(4A) *Dolphins are regarded as the friendliest creatures in the sea*
   (a) Everest/known to be/high mountain/world
   (b) Shakespeare/considered to be/great writer/English
   (c) Algae/believed to be/simple form/life

(4B) *The most common argument in favour of man's superiority is the least satisfactory*
   (a) expensive dress in the shop/attractive.
   (b) intellectual book he wrote/popular.
   (c) intelligent mammals in captivity/aggressive.

D   Similar To and Different From

Dolphins have an echo-location system which is similar to a bat's. Our aims and interests are different from dolphins' and whales'.
We can rewrite these sentences without changing the meaning – Dolphins have an echo-location system *like* a bat's. Our aims and interests are *not the same as* dolphins' and whales'. Change the following sentences, substituting *like* for *similar to* and *not the same as* for *different from*.
(1) The world is *similar to* a ball.
(2) A plane's wings are *similar to* a bird's.

(3) A squash racquet is *similar to* a tennis racquet. It is *different from* a tennis racquet because it is smaller and lighter.

(4) His work is *different from* mine.

(5) An Indian elephant is *similar to* an African elephant except that its ears are *different from* an African elephant's in shape.

E Proportional Comparisons

When two things vary to the same extent, we use the comparative form – *The more we learn about dolphins, the more we realise that they are better organised than people previously imagined.* Put the words in italics into the comparative form in the same way.

(1) The *hard* you study, the *much* you will learn.

(2) The *large* the city, the *great* the problems.

(3) The *intelligent* the species, the *complex* its organisation.

(4) The *good* you treat animals, the *good* they behave.

(5) The *much* you argue, the *bad* it will be.

F Nouns used to Represent Classes, Types, Species

When we talk about animals or things in general, we usually use the noun in the plural without 'the' – *Dolphins are more interesting than lions and tigers because they are livelier.*
It is also possible, however, to use the noun in the singular when it is representative of the type or species as a whole – *The only great whale kept in a zoo for a year learned as fast as a dolphin.* Put the following sentences into the plural.

(1) A dolphin is capable of performing tricks, like a circus animal.

(2) A dolphin's brain can transmit and receive sound and has an echo-location system, similar to a bat's.

(3) A man's interests are very different from a dolphin's.

When we refer to a species as a species, it is usual to use the definite article – *Whales, especially the smaller types, like the killer whale, are probably as intelligent as dolphins* – but there is an exception. *Man* does not take 'the' but means 'the human species' – *Some scientists claim that they are the most intelligent species in the world, apart from man.* Complete the following sentences with 'the', where necessary.

(1) The most ambitious species in the world is....man.
(2) Some species, such as....tiger and....polar bear, are in danger of becoming extinct.
(3) The most common argument in favour of....man's superiority over other species is the least satisfactory.

G Composition

Compare the following, explaining in what ways they are similar to each other and different from each other.

(1) A personal secretary, a shorthand typist and a copy typist.
(2) An architect, a surveyor and a draughtsman.
(3) Fried eggs, boiled eggs and omelettes.
(4) Football, rugby and hockey.
(5) A bear, a wolf and a dog.

PROGRESS TEST
Choose the correct alternative in each case.

London Zoo is the $\frac{\text{older}}{\text{oldest}}$ zoo in the world and has the $\frac{\text{more}}{\text{most}}$ complete collection of animals in England. They are not so well housed $\frac{\text{as}}{\text{than}}$ in $\frac{\text{more modern}}{\text{moderner}}$ zoos but recent improvements have made conditions $\frac{\text{much better}}{\text{a lot more good}}$ than they used to be. Nevertheless, the animals have $\frac{\text{much less}}{\text{much fewer}}$ freedom to move $\frac{\text{as}}{\text{than}}$ in their natural environment. One of the $\frac{\text{more}}{\text{most}}$ interesting experiments in recent years, aimed at creating a $\frac{\text{more}}{\text{most}}$ natural environment $\frac{\text{than}}{\text{as}}$ a zoo, is the safari park. Here the animals are not $\frac{\text{nearly so}}{\text{as much}}$ enclosed $\frac{\text{as}}{\text{than}}$ they are in a zoo. But safari parks are $\frac{\text{as}}{\text{like}}$ zoos because there are still fences between different species. Although lions seldom attack visitors' cars, they have the same interest in hunting deer $\frac{\text{as}}{\text{than}}$ in Africa.

Section Two

Word Order

19 Me Tarzan. You Wife. Me Boss

Tarzan is one of the few characters in fiction to have
become a folk hero and although his popularity has fallen
off since its peak in the 1920's, he is now said to be coming
back into fashion. Yet no one imagined that Tarzan would
5   become a household word when the character was first
introduced to the public.

His creator, Edgar Rice Burroughs, had had a succession
of jobs before turning to writing but they had all fallen
through. It was only when everything else had failed and
10   it seemed impossible that anyone would offer him further
employment that he fell back on fiction as a last resort.
He wrote some stories about a man on Mars *and sent them to a
publisher. He explained the incident to his readers many years
afterwards.* At first *he did not show his wife the stories*
15   because he was ashamed of such an unmanly occupation
but when the publisher paid him 400 dollars for them he
could no longer keep back the good news. *It was then that he
hit on the idea of Tarzan* and *it was Tarzan who made him a
millionaire.*

20   The Tarzan Burroughs originally wrote about is a
little different from the film hero we are used to. For one
thing, he speaks fluent English. Although educated by
apes, he is really the orphaned son of two English aristo-
crats and his way of speaking suggests to us that the apes
25   not only taught him tree-climbing and rope-swinging but
also managed to give him a public school education.

But *it was the cinema that made Tarzan famous.* For
the first film, Burroughs announced to the public that
Tarzan would kill twenty lions. He failed to keep his
30   promise but at least the hero killed one. The lion had been
given an injection to make it sleepy but it recovered
from the effects of the drug sooner than expected and the
star was obliged to stab it in self-defence. The film was a
tremendous success and from that time on *the* Hollywood
35   *studios* kept up a steady output of Tarzan adventures and
showed them to audiences all over the world.

Of course the character is absurd. Burroughs knew very

little about Africa and never troubled to visit it. Yet *we*
are still shown Tarzan films on television and our children
40   are presented with Tarzan comics as soon as they learn to
read. *What is it that gives Tarzan his tremendous appeal?*
For the adult reader, the answer is probably that Tarzan
offers the ordinary man the illusion of strength and
freedom. If his wife nags him, if his bank manager refuses
45   to lend him money, he can take refuge in a world where
there is no talk of women's liberation and keeping up with
the Joneses is not important. 'Me Tarzan. You wife. Me
boss'.

A   Comprehension

Which of the following statements is correct in the context
of the passage?

(1) Tarzan (a) is more popular than ever (b) is less
    popular than he was ten years ago (c) enjoyed his
    greatest period of success in the 1920's.
(2) Edgar Rice Burroughs began writing because (a) he
    was ashamed of his job (b) he was out of work (c) he
    thought the character of Tarzan would make him
    rich.
(3) The Tarzan Burroughs originally wrote about (a)
    was educated at a public school (b) speaks in the
    same way as the Tarzan of the films (c) lost his
    parents when he was very young.
(4) The first actor to play Tarzan (a) was attacked by a
    lion (b) killed several lions (c) had to be given an
    injection.
(5) Tarzan is still popular because (a) we learn a lot
    about Africa when we read about him (b) he helps
    men to forget their household worries (c) he is a
    dreamer.

B   Words

Choose the word or phrase from the alternatives given
which is closest in meaning to the words in italics in the
context of the passage.

(1) *Fell back on* (1.11) (a) turned to in desperation (b) collapsed on (c) tripped over.

(2) *Ashamed of* (1.15) (a) embarrassed by (b) shocked by (c) disgusted by.

(3) *Originally* (1.20) (a) at first (b) independently (c) without using the work of others.

(4) *Announced to* (1.28) (a) advised (b) warned (c) told.

(5) *Troubled* (1.38) (a) upset (b) bothered (c) worried.

(6) *Illusion* (1.43) (a) hope (b) interest (c) fantasy.

C Patterns

(1) A number of verbs can take two objects. The most common order in writing sentences with these verbs is to put the indirect object first – *He did not show his wife the stories.* Study this pattern and reproduce it, substituting the words given. Change or put in articles, possessives, prepositions where necessary.

(a) The apes/teach/Jane/tree-climbing

(b) The producer/give/the star/an injection

(c) The bank manager/lend/me/the money

(d) He/send/us/the stories

(e) The firm/offer/him/a job

There is an alternative construction where the direct object is placed first and the indirect object is used with 'to' (with some verbs 'for') – *He did not show the stories to his wife.* We prefer this second construction when we want to emphasise the indirect object – *He did not show me the stories, but he showed them to his wife.*

(2a) Reproduce this pattern, using the words supplied

(a) The apes/teach/Jane/tree-climbing/they/it/Tarzan.

(b) The producer/give/the star/an injection/he/one/the lion.

(c) The bank manager/lend/me/the money/he/it/my wife.

(d) He/send/us/the stories/he/them/a publisher.

(e) The firm/offer/him/a job/they/one/his brother.

The construction shown here is also preferred when the indirect object is rather long – *the studios showed the films to audiences all over the world.*

E

(2b) Reproduce this pattern, using the words supplied.
  (a) The dentist/give/injection/everyone who came to the surgery.
  (b) The bank manager/refuse/loans/all those who applied for them.
  (c) The author/sell/the film rights/to the company that offered most money.

(3) When a verb takes two objects in the active voice, we usually make the personal object the subject of a sentence written in the passive – *we are still shown Tarzan films on television*. The alternative construction– *Tarzan films are still shown to us* is used for emphasis – for example, if the sentence continued – *but Mickey Mouse films are not*. Make the following sentences passive. Begin the sentence with the word in italic type and do not use an agent (*by them* etc).
  (a) They gave *the lion* an injection.
  (b) They offered *me* a job in a film studio.
  (c) They taught *Tarzan* tree-climbing and rope swinging.

D   Verb + Direct object + 'To' + Indirect Object

Certain verbs can have two objects, but always follow Pattern (2), not Pattern (1). *He explained the incident to his readers many years afterwards.* Repeat this pattern in the following sentences.

(1) Burroughs/introduce/Tarzan/the public/in 1912.
(2) He/describe/what happened/his readers/in his autobiography.
(3) Burroughs/announce/the plot of the film/the public/before filming began.
(4) He/propose/a Tarzan film/Hollywood studio/soon after his first novel was published.
(5) The studio/entrust/the part of Tarzan/Johnny Weissmuller/after he had become world swimming champion.

E   'It' as Substitute Subject

(1) 'It' can be used for emphasis as a substitute subject.

Compare these sentences:
Tarzan made him a millionaire
It was Tarzan who made him a millionaire
The cinema made Tarzan famous
It was the cinema that made Tarzan famous
The meaning is the same in each case, except that the example in italics is more emphatic. Make the following sentences emphatic in the same way, using 'who' if the subject is a person, 'that' if it is a thing.

(a) Edgar Rice Burroughs created the character of Tarzan.

(b) The star killed the lion.

(c) The illusion of strength and freedom attracts male readers to Tarzan.

(2) Any part of a sentence can be emphasised in the the same way by putting 'it' at the beginning. This is commonly used with adverbs of time and place.
Then he hit on the idea of Tarzan
It was then that he hit on the idea of Tarzan
The Tarzan films were made in Hollywood
It was in Hollywood that the Tarzan films were made
Make the following sentences emphatic, using 'that'.

(a) When everything else had failed, he fell back on fiction.

(b) His popularity reached its peak in the 1920's.

(c) He learnt to train animals in Africa.

(3) The same construction is also found in questions
What gives Tarzan his tremendous appeal?
What is it that gives Tarzan his tremendous appeal?
Make the following questions emphatic, using 'that'

(a) Who started the women's liberation movement?

(b) When are you going on holiday?

(c) How have you managed to do it, when everyone else has failed?

F   Phrasal Verbs – Fall

Complete the sentences with one of the following prepositions – *back on, behind with, for, off, out* (2), *over, through*

(1) Tarzan's popularity has fallen....since the 1920's.
(2) When everything else had failed, Burroughs fell....
.... fiction.
(3) All the jobs he had fell....
(4) Everything fell....as we had planned.
(5) The hotel manager fell....himself to be polite.
(6) Tarzan fell....Jane as soon as they met.
(7) They have fallen........their rent so they will have to leave.
(8) They were so friendly. I'm surprised that they have fallen ....

G Phrasal Verbs – Keep

Complete the sentences below with one of the following prepositions – *back, on, up* (2), *up with*

(1) When the publisher bought the stories, Burroughs could not keep....the good news.
(2) He kept....working until he was over seventy.
(3) The film was a success and Hollywood kept....a steady output of Tarzan films afterwards.
(4) It costs a lot to keep .... the house.
(5) Suburban housewives spend a lot of money trying to keep .... the Joneses.

H Composition

Either (a) explain how Edgar Rice Burroughs became a millionaire or (b) explain the process by which a novel can eventually become a film.

PROGRESS TEST
Rewrite the sentences, putting the words and phrases in the correct order.
(1) He/us the stories/sent.
(2) He/to his wife/did not show/them.
(3) Him/the firm/a job/offered.
(4) Tarzan films/are shown/we/on television.
(5) Burroughs/to/Tarzan/introduced/the public.
(6) He/his readers/explained/the incident/to.

(7) The bank manager/all those who applied for them/
    loans/to/refused.
(8) Tarzan/who/was/a millionaire/it/made him.
(9) That/then/he hit on/the idea of Tarzan/it was.
(10) What/it/is/his appeal/gives Tarzan/that?

20 I Know Where I'm Going

Roger and June, old friends of George's, have invited
George and Angela to spend the weekend with them at
their house in the country. George and Angela are
driving along a country road. Angela is beginning to get
5   impatient.

ANGELA *Don't you remember where Roger's house is,* then?

GEORGE I thought I did. But now *I'm not sure if we're on the
    right road.* Perhaps we should have turned left
    at the crossroads. The trouble is that it wasn't
10   very clear which way the signpost was pointing.

ANGELA It's no use looking at me, darling. You know what
    I'm like. I can't tell left from right. But *I can't
    imagine why you didn't look up the route before we set out.*

GEORGE I thought the map was in the glove compartment.
15   But now I can't remember where I put it.

ANGELA How typical!

GEORGE Here comes someone on a bicycle. He's sure to
    know where Roger's house is. Everyone knows
    everyone else in the country. I say! (The cyclist
20   gets off his bicycle and comes round to George's
    side of the car). Do you know if this road goes
    past a house called Redgate? (The cyclist stares
    at him without saying anything).

ANGELA *Ask him if it leads to Swanbury.* The house is near
25   Swanbury, isn't it?

GEORGE Yes. Does it lead to Swanbury? (The cyclist makes

a gesture with his hands to show that he doesn't understand). He doesn't seem to know where he is, either. I say, Angela! He's carrying onions on his handlebars.

30

ANGELA *What a man!* We're lost in the middle of nowhere and he wants to know why a countryman is carrying onions. Perhaps he's going to market.

GEORGE Are you taking those onions to market?

35 CYCLIST Thirty pence. (He offers George some onions).

GEORGE (to Angela). He thinks I'm asking him how much the onions cost.

ANGELA Come on, George. There's no point in going on with this.

40 CYCLIST (taking a French passport out of his pocket and showing it to George). Onions. Thirty pence.

GEORGE Now I understand what he's doing. He's come over from France to sell onions.

ANGELA (sarcastically) *How interesting!* I don't know why you're looking so pleased about it.

45

GEORGE Well, I've solved the mystery. No wonder he doesn't know where Roger's house is. (to the cyclist). No, thank you. Merci. Merci beaucoup. (The cyclist gets on his bicycle and rides away. At the same time, a car approaches from the opposite direction and the driver stops when he sees Angela).

50

ROGER Hello, Angela! I wasn't sure how soon you'd arrive so I was going into Swanbury to buy a few things.

55

ANGELA What a relief! We were wondering if we'd ever find your house.

GEORGE (getting out of the car) What nonsense, darling! Don't take any notice of her, Roger! She always exaggerates. The house is about a mile further on the right, isn't it?

60

ROGER Actually, it's about two miles on the left. Do you think you'll be able to find it?

ANGELA (decisively) Not by ourselves, Roger. We'll follow you into Swanbury and come back with you. Frankly, I doubt if we could find our way home!

65

A Comprehension

Which of the following statements is correct in the context of the passage?

(1) George (a) turned left at the crossroads (b) turned right at the crossroads (c) went in the direction the signpost was pointing.

(2) George thought the cyclist would know where Roger's house was because (a) he was a friend of Roger's (b) he was riding a bicycle (c) people in the country usually know who their neighbours are.

(3) Angela (a) wanted to know if the cyclist was going to market (b) was surprised to see a countryman carrying onions (c) could not understand why George was interested in the onions.

(4) George was pleased because (a) he had found out where Roger's house was (b) he was proud of his French (c) he had found out why the man was carrying onions.

(5) George (a) was going in the right direction (b) was going in the wrong direction (c) knew where the house was all the time.

B Words

Choose the word or phrase from the alternatives given which is closest in meaning to the words in italics in the context of the passage.

(1) *I can't tell* (1.12) (a) I can't speak (b) I don't know the difference between (c) I can't say.

(2) *Route* (1.13) (a) way (b) main road (c) distance.

(3) *Set out* (1.13) (a) started our journey (b) made our plans (c) left the main road.

(4) *Sure* (1.17) (a) confident (b) certain (c) secure.

(5) *Past* (1.22) (a) through (b) by (c) beside.

(6) *Lead* (1.26) (a) conduct (b) guide (c) go towards.

(7) *No wonder* (1.46) (a) it's not surprising (b) it's not wonderful (c) it's not a problem.

(8) *Take any notice of* (1.59) (a) pay any attention to (b) regard (c) notice.

(9) *Actually* (1.62) (a) now (b) in fact (c) at present.
(10) *By ourselves* (1.64) (a) in our own car (b) side by side
(c) without help.

C Patterns

(1) Are we on the right road?
I'm not sure if we are on the right road
Does it lead to Swanbury?
Ask him if it leads to Swanbury

Use each of the following phrases in turn – *I'm not sure, I
wonder, Ask him* – to change the direct questions into indirect questions.
(a) Should we have turned left at the crossroads?
(b) Has the signpost been moved?
(c) Does this road go past a house called Redgate?
(d) Can she speak English?
(e) Will she be here tomorrow?

(2) Where is Roger's house?
Don't you remember where Roger's house is?
Why didn't you look up the route before we set out?
*I can't imagine why you didn't look up the route before we
set out*

Use each of the following phrases in turn – *I wonder,
I can't imagine, I don't know* – to change the direct questions
into indirect questions.
(a) Who is she?
(b) Why are you looking so pleased about it?
(c) Where did you put it?
(d) How much do the onions cost?
(e) How soon will he arrive?

D Exclamations

(1) Exclamations employing an adjective alone are
formed with 'how'– – *How interesting!* Comment on
each of the following statements using 'how' and
the most appropriate adjective of the three –
delightful, strange, typical.
(a) George has lost his way.

(b) We're going to Italy for our holiday

(c) He refused our invitation and didn't want to tell me why he couldn't come.

(2) When a noun forms part of the exclamation 'what' is used – *What a man!* If the noun is not countable, or if it is plural, the expression is formed without 'a'– *What nonsense! What children!* Use the most appropriate of these expressions – *What a pity! What a nuisance! What a relief! What nonsense! What carelessness! What weather!* – in the following sentences.

(a) 'I never lose my way', George said. 'What . . . . !' said Angela.

(b) It has been raining for three days without stopping. What . . . . !

(c) Here's Roger. What . . . . ! We were wondering if we'd ever find the house.

(d) You've made five mistakes in the same sentence. What . . . . !

(e) The train is late again. What . . . . !

(f) Their little boy is ill, so he won't be able to come to the children's party. What . . . . !

(3) Frequently adjectives and nouns are joined in exclamations. In such cases 'what' is used – *What a pretty dress! What disgusting behaviour! What comfortable chairs!* Use the most appropriate of these expressions – *What a wonderful idea! – What an awful shock! – What a pleasant surprise! – What helpful people! – What beautiful flowers! – What expensive clothes!* in the following sentences.

(1) I didn't expect to see you here. I'm so glad you were able to come. What . . . . !

(2) What . . . . ! I wish I could afford them.

(3) When she arrived from work, she found that her flat had been burgled. What . . . . !

(4) What . . . . ! You must spend a lot of time looking after your garden.

(5) Let's celebrate the good news by going out to dinner. What . . . . !

(6) What ....! We would never have found our way without their assistance.

E   Prepositions with Vehicles

Complete the sentences with the correct preposition – *into*, *off, on* (2), *out, out of*.
(1) The cyclist got .... his bicycle and rode away.
(2) George got .... the car and went to meet Roger.
(3) Get .... the bus at the corner and get .... at the town centre.
(4) If you get .... the car I'll give you a lift.
(5) Take the train from Victoria and get .... at Clapham Junction.

F   Composition

(1) A foreigner who does not speak your language very well asks you to help him to find the way to a place in your city. You do not know it yourself but take him to a policeman and act as an interpreter. Write a dialogue with the policeman in which he asks you what the foreigner wants to know.
(2) You are walking along the street with a deaf relative. A stranger stops you and asks for information. The relative is curious and continually wants to know what the stranger is asking you. Write the dialogue.

PROGRESS TEST
Rewrite the following sentences, putting the words and phrases in the correct order.
(1) I can't/I put it/remember/where.
(2) He's sure/Roger's house/is/where/to know.
(3) Do/this road/if/you know/a house called Redgate/goes past?
(4) The house/isn't it/near Swanbury/is?
(5) He wants/a countryman/why/onions/is carrying/to know.
(6) What/I understand/he/doing/is.
(7) I'm asking him/cost/the onions/how much.

(8) George/the car/of/out/got.
(9) What/people/helpful!
(10) Surprise/a/what/pleasant!

21 The News of the Village

Visitors to Britain are sometimes surprised to learn that
newspapers there have such a large circulation. *The
'quality' newspapers are often held up as an example* of impartial
journalism but the 'Daily Mirror' and the 'Daily Express'
5   usually impress newspapermen even more because they
both sell about four million copies every day. *British
families generally buy a newspaper every morning* and frequently take two or three on Sundays but the vast
circulation figures obtained are not only due to the
10   Englishman's thirst for news. Because the newspapers are
all published nationally, copies can be delivered everywhere at the same time.
    Though people abroad often know the names of the
national papers, they seldom realise that there is another
15   branch of the British press which sells almost as many
copies. Local newspapers have a weekly circulation of
13 million. Almost every town and country area has one.
Nearly all of them hold their own financially and many
of them are very profitable.
20   These papers are written almost entirely for readers
interested in local events – births, weddings, deaths,
council meetings and sport – but the content is naturally
influenced by the kind of community they serve. Editors
prefer to rely on a small staff of people who all know the
25   district well. A great deal of local news is regularly
supplied by clubs and churches in the neighbourhood and
it does not get out of date as quickly as national news.
If there is no room for it in this week's edition, *an item can
sometimes be held over until the following week.*

30   The editor must never forget that the success of any
newspaper depends on advertising. He is usually anxious
to keep the good will of local businessmen for this reason.
But if the newspaper is well written and the news items
have been carefully chosen to attract local readers, the
35   businessmen are grateful for the opportunity to keep
their products in the public eye.
    Local newspapers do not often comment on problems of
national importance and editors rarely hold with taking
sides on political questions. But *they can often be of service*
40   *to the community* in expressing public feeling on local issues.
A newspaper can sometimes persuade the council to take action to
provide better shopping facilities, improve transport in
the area and preserve local monuments and places of
interest.
45   These papers often sound rather dull and it seems
surprising that they all make a profit. But for many
people in small towns and villages the death of someone
known to them or the installation of traffic lights at a
busy corner nearby can sometimes be more important
50   than a disaster in a foreign country.

A   Comprehension

Which of the following statements is correct in the
context of the passage?

  (1) The 'Daily Mirror' and the 'Daily Express' usually
      impress newspapermen from abroad because they
      (a) are impartial (b) have a large circulation
      (c) are 'quality' newspapers.
  (2) Newspapers have a large circulation in Britain
      because (a) British families read two or three
      every day (b) they are patriotic (c) copies are sold
      all over the country.
  (3) Local newspaper editors (a) only employ people who
      live in the neighbourhood (b) rely entirely on clubs
      and churches for news (c) like to employ journalists
      with a knowledge of local affairs.
  (4) Local newspapers are usually successful because (a)
      they attract advertisements from local businessmen

(b) the editors give businessmen presents (c) they deal with political questions.

(5) Local newspapers (a) frequently change sides on political questions (b) are mainly concerned with what happens in the neighbourhood (c) often provide local amenities.

B Words

Choose the word or phrase from the alternatives given which is closest in meaning to the words in italics in the context of the passage.

(1) *Held up* (1.3) (a) exposed (b) suspended (c) exhibited.
(2) *Take* (1.8) (a) steal (b) carry (c) buy.
(3) *Vast* (1.8) (a) wasteful (b) enormous (c) grand.
(4) *Abroad* (1.13) (a) foreign (b) overseas (c) on the Continent.
(5) *A great deal* (1.25) (a) a large number (b) several (c) a large amount.
(6) *Get out of date* (1.27) (a) lose its interest as news (b) get published on the wrong day (c) become old-fashioned.
(7) *Held over* (1.29) (a) maintained (b) suspended (c) retained for use.
(8) *Rarely* (1.38) (a) very seldom (b) unusually (c) strangely.
(9) *Issues* (1.40) (a) results (b) matters for discussion (c) editions.
(10) *Sound* (1.45) (a) listen (b) seem (c) noise.

C Patterns

Study the pattern italicised in each case and then reproduce it, substituting the words given but taking care to form the verbs correctly. Change or put in articles, possessives, prepositions where necessary. Put the adverb in brackets in the correct position to complete the pattern.

(1a) *British families generally buy a newspaper every morning*

(a) Editors/employ/people/from the same district (usually).

(b) Local businessmen/put/advertisements/in the local paper (frequently).

(c) A company/keep/products/in the public eye (always).

(d) The editor/write/editorial/on a political question (seldom).

(e) Local newspapers/produce/improvements/in shopping facilities (sometimes).

(1b) *Local newspapers do not often comment on problems of national importance*

(a) I/reply to/letters asking for money (usually).

(b) Editors/rely on/clubs and churches for news (always).

(c) Local newspapers/deal with/items of local news (always).

(2a) *The 'quality' newspapers are often held up as an example*

(a) Readers' letters/publish/in local newspapers (frequently).

(b) Decisions/take/at council meetings (usually).

(c) Journalists/pay/by the month (normally).

(d) A local newspaper/write/for local people (generally).

(e) The matriculation fee/return/to students (rarely).

(2b) *An item can sometimes be held over until the following week*

(a) Councils/can/persuade/to change their minds (occasionally).

(b) He/will/remember/as a great man (always).

(c) I/have/employ/on a local newspaper (never).

(3a) *A newspaper can sometimes persuade the council to take action*

(a) I/could/ask her/to return the ring (never).

(b) I/have/tell him/to work harder (frequently).

(c) The editor/must/remind his staff/to encourage advertising (always).

(d) He/may/want you/to take shorthand (occasionally).

(3b) *They can often be of service to the community*

(a) They/can/a nuisance to people (sometimes).

(b) A newspaper/should/interesting to its readers (always).

(c) He/has/afraid to speak the truth (never).

D Adverbs of Manner in Passive Constructions

Adverbs of manner are usually placed between the verb '*be*' and the past participle in passive constructions – *if his newspaper is well written and the news items have been carefully chosen to attract local readers*. Put the verbs in brackets in the normal position in the following sentences.

(a) The film is made (badly).

(b) The report has been complied (carefully).

(c) The book was produced (expensively).

(d) The staff have been trained (properly).

(e) You will be rewarded (generously).

E Both and All

(1) *They both sell over four million copies*

Notice the position of 'both' in this sentence and note that it could be rewritten: 'Both of them sell over four million copies'. Change the following sentences in the same way.

(1) They both work for the 'Daily Express'.

(2) We both live in the neighbourhood.

(3) They both make a profit.

Now rewrite each sentence, substituting 'all' for 'both'.

(2) *The newspapers are all published nationally*

Notice the position of 'all' in this sentence and note that it could be rewritten: 'All the newspapers are published nationally'. Change the following sentences in the same way.

(1) The journalists are all employed locally.

(2) Newspapers are all dependent on advertising.

(3) Local papers are all written for local people.

(3) *All his books have been published in Britain*
All the tickets will be sold before we get there

Notice that these sentences could be rewritten: *His books*

have all been published in Britain. The tickets will all be sold before we get there. Change the following sentences in the same way.

    (1) All the journalists have been paid.
    (2) All our money has been spent.
    (3) All your efforts may be wasted.
    (4) Both my letters were published in the local paper.
    (5) All local events will be fully reported.

F   Phrasal Verbs – Hold

Fill in the blanks in the sentences with one of the following – *off, out, over, their own, up*(3), *with*

    (1) The 'quality' newspapers are often held .... as an example of impartial journalism.
    (2) A news item can sometimes be held .... until the following week.
    (3) Nearly all local newspapers hold .... financially.
    (4) Do you think the rain will hold .... until we get home?
    (5) Editors of local newspapers rarely hold .... taking sides on political questions.
    (6) The train was held .... by fog.
    (7) I don't think our supplies will hold .... much longer.
    (8) The bank robbers held .... a train.

G   Composition

(a) Which newspaper do you usually buy and what subjects are regularly covered in it? Describe the content of the newspaper and say why you buy it in preference to any other newspaper you know.

(b) Answer the same question with reference to a magazine.

PROGRESS TEST
Put the words and phrases in the correct order.
    (1) The editor/editorials/seldom/on a political question/ writes.

(2) Rely on/always/do not/for news/editors/clubs.
(3) Local people/written/is/for/generally/a local newspaper.
(4) A great man/he/always/will/as/be remembered.
(5) The truth/has/never/he/been afraid/to speak.
(6) I/to work harder/him/told/frequently/have.
(7) Made/the film/badly/is.
(8) You/generously/rewarded/will be.
(9) Local papers/all/for local people/written/are. (2
possibilities)
(10) All/have/the journalists/been paid. (2 possibilities)
(11) Both/four million copies/sell/they.
(12) Of them/four million copies/both/sell.

22 A Break in the Routine

Jonathan Rivers lived alone in a neat, two-storey, semi-
detached house in Compton Street. Like many bachelors
approaching middle age, he was getting rather set in his
ways. He caught the same train to London every morning,
5   ate his lunch in the same crowded restaurant near the
office where he worked and always came home on the
6.00 train. People were so used to seeing Jonathan set
off at a quarter past eight, dressed in a simple dark suit,
wearing a black bowler hat and carrying a rolled umbrella
10   on his arm, that they said you didn't need to wear a
watch if you lived in Compton Street.
   Ever since Jonathan had set up house in Compton
Street, he had looked after it very carefully. *He worked
hard in the garden every Sunday* and set out to impress the
15   neighbours with his flower beds and lawn. Before he left
the house in the mornings, he carefully closed all the
doors downstairs, opened some windows to let the air in
and locked the front door. Everything Jonathan did
was tidy and systematic.

F

20   One summer evening *Jonathan returned home as usual
at five minutes to seven* precisely. When he opened the
front gate he immediately noticed something strange.
There was a heavy footprint in the earth in one of the
flower beds. Jonathan was just going to blame the milk-
25   man or the postman when he noticed that one of the
white lace curtains in the front room downstairs was
out of place. Jonathan never left anything out of place.
    He walked up to the front door and opened it quietly.
He listened carefully for a few moments but could hear
30   nothing. The front-room door was half-open. Jonathan
studied it thoughtfully, wondering if he had forgotten to
close it that morning. He had never forgotten before. He
stepped silently across the hall to the door and looked
inside the room. The shadow of a man was clearly
35   reflected on the far wall in the evening sunlight. He had
obviously been standing behind the door since Jonathan's
return. Jonathan grabbed the door-handle, slammed the
door and turned the key. Then *he calmly picked up the
telephone* in the hall and set about calling the police.
40   The burglar, a tall, thick-set, bearded fellow, tried to
climb through a window to get out but Jonathan had
expected that. He set about him with his umbrella,
using it like a sword. *Three minutes later the police arrived
on the scene.* Jonathan was a little annoyed that he had
45   to have dinner later than usual but on the whole he
felt quite pleased with himself.

A   Comprehension

Which of the following statements is correct in the context
of the passage?

(1) Jonathan was (a) an old bachelor (b) a single man
    (c) a widower.
(2) Before leaving the house Jonathan closed (a) all the
    doors (b) all the windows (c) all the doors and
    windows.
(3) Jonathan first realised that someone might be in
    the house because (a) he saw a footprint (b) the

front door was open (c) there was something wrong with the curtains.

(4) Jonathan realised the burglar was in the front room because (a) the door was open (b) he saw the man's shadow (c) he saw the man standing behind the door.

(5) Jonathan was able to prevent the burglar from escaping because (a) he had a sword (b) he was bigger and stronger (c) he was carrying an umbrella.

B Words

Choose the word or phrase from the alternatives given which is closest in meaning to the words in italics in the context of the passage.

(1) *Two-storey* (1.1) (a) consisting of two floors (b) consisting of two flats (c) having two separate entrances.

(2) *Set in his ways* (1.3) (a) taking the same route to the office every day (b) fixed in his habits and routine (c) established in the neighbourhood.

(3) *Didn't need to* (1.10) (a) didn't have to (b) weren't to (c) shouldn't.

(4) *Set out* (1.14) (a) went out into the garden (b) laid out the garden (c) deliberately tried.

(5) *Tidy* (1.19) (a) neat (b) monotonous (c) repetitive.

(6) *Precisely* (1.21) (a) exactly (b) necessarily (c) inevitably.

(7) *Far* (1.35) (a) distant (b) opposite (c) facing.

(8) *Slammed* (1.37) closed (a) slowly (b) quickly (c) silently.

(9) *Thick-set* (1.40) (a) fat (b) unintelligent (c) heavily built.

(10) *The police* (1.43) (a) a policeman (b) the local policeman (c) some policemen.

C Patterns

(1) *He calmly picked up the telephone*
Adverbs often appear between the subject and the verb, instead of coming after the object, when the adverb is a

single word. This emphasises the adverb rather more than 'He picked up the telephone calmly'. Put the adverb in the emphatic position in these sentences.

(a) He closed all the doors carefully.

(b) He noticed something strange immediately.

(c) He opened the gate quietly.

(d) She refused the offer firmly.

(e) I learned the truth about the matter gradually.

(2) *He worked hard in the garden every Sunday*

When there is more than one adverb in a sentence we usually follow the order *how* (hard), *where* (in the garden), *when* (every Sunday). Put the adverbs in brackets in the correct order in the sentence, following this pattern.

(a) He had lunch (at home, alone, at 1.o'clock).

(b) He listened (outside the door, for a few moments, carefully).

(c) They plan to get married (tomorrow, at St. Mary's church, quietly).

(d) I'll read the report (after lunch, in my office, in detail).

(e) We'll decide the matter (at the meeting, democratically, next week).

NOTE See (3) and (4) for variations in this order.

(3) *Jonathan returned home as usual at five minutes to seven*

When a number of adverbs occur in a sentence following a verb of movement, we are usually most interested in *where* someone was going etc., so the order *where* (home), *how* (as usual), *when* (at five minutes to seven) is most common in such cases. Put the adverbs in brackets in the correct order in the sentence, following this pattern.

(a) They are arriving (this evening, in London, by plane).

(b) I sent the order (by express mail, yesterday, to the customer).

(c) He travels (by train, every day, to London).

(d) The bridegroom arrived (five minutes after the bride, in a hurry, at the church).

(e) They're coming (tomorrow, to the office, for a meeting).

(4) *Three minutes later the police arrived on the scene*
Instead of placing the adverb of time at the end of a
series, we can put it before the subject. We could write
this sentence – *The police arrived on the scene three minutes
later.* We use this order most frequently when there
are a large number of adverbs in a sentence – *One
summer evening* (when), *Jonathan returned home* (where),
as usual (how) *at five minutes to seven* (when). Rewrite
these sentences, putting the adverb of time before the
subject.

    (a) He listened carefully outside the door for a few
        moments.
    (b) I'll read the report in detail in my office after
        lunch.
    (c) He travels to London by train every day.
    (d) The burglar quickly jumped through the window
        as soon as he saw Jonathan.
    (e) He carefully closed all the doors downstairs
        before he left the house.

D Adjective Position

Put the adjectives in brackets in the most normal position
and order in each sentence.

(1) One of the curtains was out of place. (lace, white)
(2) He was dressed in a suit. (dark, simple).
(3) Jonathan lived in a house in Compton Street.
    (two-storey, neat).
(4) I bought a carpet. (Persian, old, beautiful).
(5) We are looking for a secretary. (English-speaking
    experienced).

E Carry and Wear

Choose the correct verb in each of the following sentences
and put it in the correct form.

(1) The bride .... a white dress and .... a bouquet of
    flowers. The bridesmaids .... blue.

(2) You didn't need to .... a watch if you lived in Compton Street.

(3) Jonathan always .... a black bowler hat and .... an umbrella.

(4) She has hundreds of dresses but she is always asking me what to .....

(5) The gypsy .... bright clothes. He .... a scarf on his head and large earrings in his ears and .... a stick.

F   Phrasal Verbs – Set

Complete the sentences with one of the following pre-positions – *about* (2), *aside*, *off* (3), *out* (2), *to*, *up*.

(1) People were used to seeing Jonathan set .... at a quarter past eight every morning.

(2) He set .... to impress the neighbours with his flower beds and lawn.

(3) We are setting .... a branch office in Canada.

(4) Jonathan picked up the telephone and set .... calling the police.

(5) When the burglar tried to escape, Jonathan set .... him with his umbrella.

(6) When the burglar entered the house, he set .... the alarm.

(7) The rings were set .... in the jeweller's window.
When the children had gone home after the party, I set .... and cleared up the mess.
Jonathan has set .... some money for his old age.
The bright wallpaper sets .... the pale carpet.

G   Composition

(1) You arrived home to find that your house had been burgled. Describe what you saw.

(2) Describe a wedding you went to.

(3) Someone passes your house every morning. Describe how he is dressed and say where you think he is going.

PROGRESS TEST

Put the words and phrases in the correct order. In the first six examples there are two possibilities. Answer each in both possible ways.

(1) He/all the doors/carefully/closed.

(2) Hard/in the garden/worked/every Sunday/he.

(3) He/outside the door/carefully/for a few moments/ listened.

(4) The report/after lunch/I'll/in detail/read/in my office.

(5) About the matter/I/the truth/gradually/learned.

(6) Arrived/on the scene/three minutes later/the police.

(7) A/suit/he/dark/was dressed in/simple.

(8) I/Persian/old/bought/a/beautiful/carpet.

(9) Was/fellow/a/thick-set/tall/the burglar/bearded.

(10) Was/Jonathan/systematic/everything/and/tidy/did.

Section Three

Relative, Noun and Adverbial Clauses

23 His Bark is Worse than His Bite

JACKIE Good morning. The agency that sent me told me to report to Miss Clark.

MISS CLARK I'm Miss Clark. *You must be the temporary we asked for.* I'm afraid *the job I've got for you* 5 *won't be easy.*

JACKIE Never mind. I like having plenty to do. At the last office I went to *I ran out of work after a couple of hours, which made the rest of the day rather boring.*

10 MISS CLARK *That's not the reason why I said the job wasn't easy.* The reason is Mr Barker, the man whose secretary is away. I don't like running down members of the staff but *he's the rudest man I've ever met.* Jane Cobb, his present 15 secretary, is the only person in the office who can stand him.

JACKIE I've run up against all kinds of people, working as a temporary. The only trouble I've ever had was with someone who *wasn't* 20 interested in my typing. *The ones who shout at me don't bother me.*

MISS CLARK (drily) If you can see the day through with Mr Barker without losing your temper, I'll believe you. I'll show you his office and 25 introduce you to him.

(In Mr Barker's office there are papers all over his desk. The filing cabinets are all open and in disorder and there is a large file on the secretary's chair facing the desk).

30 MISS CLARK This is Miss Curtis. She'll be seeing to your correspondence while Miss Cobb's away.

MR BARKER Does she come from the agency that sent the last temporary I had? That girl couldn't take things down in longhand, let alone 35 shorthand. All right, Miss Clark. (She goes out and he speaks to Jackie). You'd better sit down, I suppose.

	JACKIE	(picking up the file from the chair) Where would you like me to put this?
40	MR BARKER	How should I know? Put it where you like. (Jackie puts it on his desk and sits down). Not on my desk! How can I work with all these papers everywhere? *Didn't they teach you common sense as well as typing at the school*
45		*where you studied? I'm looking forward to the day when Miss Cobb comes back,* I can tell you.
	JACKIE	I imagine you're not the only one, Mr Barker.
	MR BARKER	The only what?
50	JACKIE	The only person who's looking forward to Miss Cobb's return.
	MR BARKER	Why is that?
	JACKIE	Because *a man whose manners are as bad as yours must try everyone's patience.*
55	MR BARKER	(picking up the phone) Miss Clark! Come and see this girl out. No, wait a minute. I'll ring you back. (He puts the phone down). Do you know, girl, that you're the first secretary I've ever had who stood up to me?
60	JACKIE	But probably I'll be the last, which is a pity. My name's not 'girl', either. It's Miss Curtis. (She gets up to leave)
	MR BARKER	No, sit down. You can't expect a man to change his habits at once, girl. But at least
65		you've seen through me, I'll say that for you. *The* only *thing that impresses me is directness.* Sit down again and take a letter . . . Miss Curtis.

A Comprehension

Which of the following statements is correct in the context of the passage?

(1) The job Jackie is required to do won't be easy because (a) she will soon run out of work (b) it will only be temporary (c) the man she will have to work for is rude.

(2) Jackie (a) is never worried by people shouting at her (b) has had a lot of trouble while working as a temporary (c) had trouble with someone because of her typing.

(3) Mr Barker (a) wanted Jackie to put the file away in its proper place (b) isn't capable of arranging his papers properly when his regular secretary is away (c) put the file on the chair to make Jackie feel uncomfortable.

(4) Mr Barker (a) is surprised that Jackie stands up when she speaks to him (b) asks Miss Clark to help Jackie find her way round the office (c) is surprised that Jackie shows independence.

(5) Jackie (a) is sorry that she will be the last secretary Mr Barker has (b) is sorry that she wasn't his first secretary (c) doesn't think other girls will talk to him as she has done.

B Words

Choose the word or phrase from the alternatives given which is closest in meaning to the words in italics in the context of the passage.

(1) *Never mind* (1.6) (a) that doesn't matter (b) don't think about it (c) you mustn't take any notice

(2) *Boring* (1.9) (a) dull (b) tiring (c) tired

(3) *Running down* (1.12) (a) knocking over (b) chasing (c) criticizing

(4) *Rudest* (1.14) (a) least sophisticated (b) clumsiest (c) worst-mannered.

(5) *Stand* (1.16) (a) put up with (b) support (c) stand up to

(6) *Run up against* (1.17) (a) crashed into (b) met (c) competed with

(7) *Seeing to* (1.30) (a) looking after (b) looking at (c) looking for

(8) *Try* (1.54) (a) attempt (b) prove (c) test

C Patterns

Study the pattern in italic type in each case and then reproduce it, substituting the words supplied. Make sure that the verbs are in the correct tense and form and put in articles, possessives, prepositions where necessary.

(1) *The ones who shout at me don't bother me*
   (a) salesmen/deal with him/trust
   (b) girls/work for him/like
   (c) people/complain about her/understand

(2) *The thing that impresses me is directness*
   (a) job/bores her/filing
   (b) firm/uses them/Grossleys
   (c) game/interests him/chess

(3) *A man whose manners are as bad as yours must try everyone's patience.*
   (a) income/is/large/his/pay very high taxes
   (b) work/is/careless/his/cost the firm a lot of money
   (c) car/is/fast/his/drive very carefully

(4A) *The job I've got for you won't be easy*
   (a) holiday/planned/us/expensive
   (b) letter/written/them/welcome
   (c) present/bought/her/surprise

(4B) *He's the rudest man I've ever met*
   (a) She/pretty/girl/seen
   (b) It/boring/book/read
   (c) It/different/job/had

(4C) *You must be the temporary we asked for*
   (a) He/man/spoke to
   (b) That/programme/listened to
   (c) That/firm/wrote to

D Co-ordinate Relative Clauses

I ran out of work after a couple of hours, which made the rest of the day rather boring
In this sentence, *which* does not refer to *hours* but to the whole of the previous clause. We could rewrite this

sentence 'I ran out of work after a couple of hours *and this* (*that*) made the rest of the day rather boring.' Use *which* as a link in the following sentences in place of *and this* (*that*).

(1) Probably I'll be the last secretary who'll stand up to you, *and that* is a pity.
(2) He was very bad-mannered, *and this* annoyed her.
(3) She couldn't take shorthand, *and that* slowed down the work of the office.
(4) He finally called her Miss Curtis, *and that* pleased her.
(5) He blamed her for the papers on his desk, *and that* was unfair.

E   Relative Adverbs

Where, when and *why* may be used to introduce relative clauses in phrases like 'the place where', 'the time when', 'the reason why'.
Didn't they teach you common-sense as well as typing at the school where you studied?
I am looking forward to the day when Miss Cobb comes back
That's not the reason why I said the job wasn't easy
Use the correct relative adverb to complete the following sentences.

(1) I was born in the street .... you live.
(2) Please report to the office on the day .... you begin work.
(3) The factory .... he works is at the end of this road.
(4) That isn't the reason .... she was late.
(5) This is the cabinet .... the files are kept.

F   Phrasal Verbs – Run

Complete the sentences with one of the following – *away with, down* (2), *into, out of, over, to, up against.*

(1) We've run .... beer, which is a nuisance.
(2) I've never run .... such a rude man.
(3) I don't like running .... other members of staff, but he deserves it.

(4) Don't run .... the idea that this job will be easy.
(5) I ran .... her quite by chance as I was walking along the street.
(6) I'm afraid we can't run .... paying him such a high salary.
(7) She needs a rest. She is run .... after working for Mr Barker.
(8) He ran .... the main points in the letter instead of dictating the whole of it to her.

G Phrasal Verbs – See

Complete the sentences with one of the following – *about, off, out, through* (2), *to*.

(1) If you can see the day .... with Mr Barker without losing your temper, I'll believe you.
(2) She'll be seeing .... your correspondence while Miss Cobb's away.
(3) See this girl ..... I've had enough of her.
(4) You've seen .... me. My bark's not as bad as my bite.
(5) We're going to see them .... at the station.
(6) It's nearly dinner time. I must see .... laying the table.

H Composition

(1) You have applied for a job and been asked to attend an interview. When you arrive, the secretary who speaks to you says she knows nothing about it. Write the dialogue in which the situation is explained.
(2) You arrive at a station and see that a train is just leaving. A porter tells you that it is the train you want. Write the dialogue and also the dialogue with another passenger on the train when you discover that it is the wrong one.

PROGRESS TEST
Complete the sentences with the correct relative pronoun

or relative adverb where necessary but make contact clauses wherever possible.

I don't know if the agency .... sent you told you about this job. We are the kind of firm .... deals with important people, ... means that anyone .... we employ must be exceptional. That is the reason .... we asked the agency to send us the best girls .... they had. The girl .... we are looking for is someone .... not only knows shorthand and typing but .... manners and dress sense are perfect. The office .... she will work is next to Mr Barker's. Any questions?

Yes. Will the man .... I work for be as well-mannered and well-dressed as I am?

24 In the Shadow of Etna

People who live on the slopes of an active volcano know that at any moment everything they possess, their homes and the crops they have carefully cultivated, may be swept away by molten lava that runs down the
5   mountainside after an eruption. When Mount Etna, which is considered to be one of Sicily's main tourist attractions, erupted in 1971 few of those who came to watch were capable of appreciating the feelings of the farmers whose homes and land were threatened.
10   *Etna, which is the most continuously active volcano in Europe, had erupted twice before in this century.* The eruption of 1928, which was the more destructive of the two, engulfed a huge area of farmland and a small town. *The villagers, who must have realised that the same thing would happen again*
15   and *whose homes were in constant danger, nevertheless hoped that the volcano would leave them in peace.*

The most dangerous volcanoes are the explosive type, one of which is Mont Pelée on the island of Martinique, which *blew up in 1902 and killed* all but one of *the inhabitants* of the

20   town *of St. Pierre, most of whom were poisoned by its noxious gases.* The only survivor was a prisoner in the town gaol whose cell was so badly ventilated that the gas did not reach him. Nowadays, instruments that can read the signs of an approaching explosion are used in populated
25   areas around such volcanoes to warn people of changes in temperature that may indicate an eruption.

    Etna, which belongs to a less dangerous category of volcanoes, called 'effusive', possessed no instruments, since it had never shown explosive tendencies. The lava
30   that has brought so much destruction in the past eventually produces good soil and so the people who lived near it were prepared to go on taking the risk.

    The mountain, which continually throws lava blocks high into the air, showed signs of a coming eruption in
35   April 1971 by suddenly becoming silent. The molten lava, trying to find a way out, forced its way through a fault in the mountain only three miles from the start of the cultivated land. The farmers whose crops were threatened could only watch patiently as the slow stream
40   of lava gradually poured down the mountainside. The land they had worked on, which was buried underneath, will not be fit for farming again for fifty years.

A   Comprehension

Which of the following statements is correct in the context of the passage?

(1) People who live near an active volcano (a) are worried about being swept away by lava (b) are always in danger of losing their homes and crops (c) run down the mountainside after an eruption.

(2) When Mount Etna erupted in 1971 (a) it became an important tourist attraction (b) everyone was concerned about the farmers who lost their homes (c) it was difficult for sightseers to understand how farmers felt about it.

(3) In the twentieth century, Etna has erupted (a) continuously (b) twice (c) three times.

(4) The villagers (a) believed the volcano would not

erupt again (b) gave up cultivating the land because
their homes were in constant danger (c) went on
cultivating the land in the hope that the eruption
would not affect them.

(5) When Mont Pelée exploded (a) almost everyone in
St. Pierre was blown up (b) a prisoner in the town
gaol was poisoned (c) almost everyone in St. Pierre
was killed by the after-effects of the explosion.

(6) (a) All populated areas now have instruments that
predict volcanic explosions (b) We know that
volcanoes erupt whenever there is a change in
temperature (c) It is now possible to know in
advance that a volcano is likely to erupt.

(7) The people who lived near Etna did not move away
because (a) they did not believe the volcano would
erupt again (b) the land near the volcano was better
for cultivation than in other places (c) they had
nowhere to go.

(8) People suspected that Etna was going to erupt
because (a) volcanic activity stopped for a time
(b) lava blocks were thrown in the air (c) a fault in
the mountain was discovered.

B Words

Choose the word or phrase from the alternatives given
which is closest in meaning to the word in italics in the
context of the passage.

(1) *Appreciating* (1.8) (a) valuing (b) understanding
(c) gaining.

(2) *Threatened* (1.9) (a) in danger (b) warned (c)
destroyed.

(3) *Leave them in peace* (1.16) (a) stop erupting (b) have a
rest (c) not affect their lives.

(4) *But* (1.19) (a) except (b) however (c) yet.

(5) *Populated areas* (1.24) (a) places which attract
tourists (b) places where a large number of people
live (c) pleasant places to live in.

(6) *Showed signs of* (1.34) (a) demonstrated (b) indicated
(c) forecast.

(7) *Fault* (1.37) (a) mistake (b) error (c) geological weakness.

(8) *Fit* (1.42) (a) suitable (b) healthy (c) sufficient.

C Patterns

Non-defining Relative Clauses are a means of expressing two separate ideas about the same person or thing in the same sentence. Instead of writing – The villagers must have realized that the same thing would happen again. Nevertheless they hoped that the volcano would leave them in peace – we can write: *The villagers, who must have realized that the same thing would happen again, nevertheless hoped that the volcano would leave them in peace.*

In each of the following exercises, use the relative pronoun (*who, which* etc.) in the example to link together the two sentences in place of the word in italic type.

(1) (a) The tourists had only come to see the spectacle of the eruption. *They* found it difficult to understand the farmers' feelings.

   (b) Journalists on local papers must know the district well to do their job. *They* are therefore local men in most cases.

   (c) The editor is not interested in politics. *He* doesn't like writing editorials.

(2) *Etna, which is the most continuously active volcano in Europe, had erupted twice before in this century.*

   (a) The eruption of 1928 was the more destructive of the two. *It* engulfed a huge area of farmland.

   (b) The mountain continually throws lava blocks high into the air. *It* showed signs of a coming eruption in April 1971.

   (c) Etna is considered to be one of Sicily's main tourist attractions. *It* erupted in 1971.

(3) *The villagers, whose homes were in constant danger, hoped that the volcano would leave them in peace.*

Note that in this group of sentences, the sentence con-

taining the possessive adjective (*his*, *their* etc.) will form
the clause between commas.

(a) Columbus reached America in October 1492. *His* voyage of discovery had been financed by Isabella of Spain.

(b) The managing director has decided to retire. *His* health has been poor for several years.

(c) Fred Smith and Tom Taylor will box again for the World Heavyweight Championship next month. *Their* last fight ended in a draw.

(4) *Mont Pelée blew up in 1902 and killed the inhabitants of St. Pierre, most of whom were poisoned by its noxious gases.*

(a) The disaster has caused great suffering among the farmers. All of *them* have lost their crops.

(b) The closing of the factory will be opposed by the employees. Many of *them* have worked there all their lives.

(c) They had two sons. Both of *them* afterwards became famous.

(5) *The most dangerous volcanoes are the explosive type, one of which is Mont Pelée on the island of Martinique.*

(a) He has a valuable collection of pictures. Some of *them* have been lent to the National Gallery.

(b) His father left him a lot of land. Most of *it* was buried under the lava.

(c) There are a number of active volcanoes in Europe. One of *them* is Mount Etna in Sicily.

D   More and Most

Choose which word is correct in order to complete each of the sentences below.

(1) Etna is the .... active volcano in Europe.

(2) The eruption of 1928 was .... destructive than that of 1950.

(3) .... of the inhabitants of St. Pierre were poisoned when Mont Pelée exploded in 1902.

(4) The .... dangerous volcanoes are the explosive type.

    (5) Which of the two main categories of volcanoes is considered .... dangerous?

    (6) .... people are fortunately free from the worries of those who live on the slopes of an active volcano.

    (7) .... of the people who came to watch the eruption did so out of curiosity.

    (8) Those who suffered .... from the eruption were the farmers who lived nearby but some farmers suffered .... than others.

    (9) .... people have read about Mount Etna than have visited it.

  (10) The .... dangerous of the two volcanoes we have been talking about was Mont Pelée.

E Collocations (1)

Complete the sentences with one of the following – *at, in, on, out of*.

    (1) None of the other planets in our solar system is capable of supporting life .... present.

    (2) I didn't like them .... first but eventually we became friends.

    (3) 'The flat is .... fire!' I shouted. 'Ring the fire brigade'.

    (4) If we haven't got a record .... stock, try to interest the customer in a different one.

    (5) San Simeon looks like a mediaeval castle but .... fact it was built for William Randolph Hearst.

    (6) My wife and children are away .... holiday so I'm alone here .... the moment.

    (7) The public can't always tell the difference .... quality but they can always recognise a difference .... price.

    (8) Dolphins are more willing to co-operate with the trainer than other mammals .... captivity.

    (9) Jonathan never left anything .... place.

  (10) He had to have dinner later than usual but .... the whole he felt quite pleased with himself.

F Composition

(1) Describe what happened when Etna erupted in 1971. (2) Draw a family tree for yourself and explain the relationships between your immediate ancestors and any interesting facts about them. (3) Give an account of the main mountain ranges and/or rivers in your country.

PROGRESS TEST
Complete the sentences with the correct relative pronoun only where one is required.

    (1) People .... live near an active volcano, ... may erupt at any moment, know that everything .... they own may be destroyed by molten lava. Those .... came to watch the eruption of Mount Etna in 1971 may have wondered why the farmers .... homes were in danger remained on the land. Etna, ... belongs to the 'effusive' category of volcanoes, had erupted twice before, but the lava .... has so often brought destruction also produces good soil for the crops .... the farmers grow.

    (2) Mont Pelée in Martinique, ... exploded in 1902, killed 30,000 people in St. Pierre, most of .... were poisoned. The only man .... escaped was a prisoner .... cell was so badly ventilated that the poisonous gas .... killed the other inhabitants did not reach him. The most dangerous volcanoes are the explosive type, many of .... now have instruments nearby .... warn people of changes in temperature .... may save their lives although the houses .... they own and the crops .... they cultivate may be destroyed.

25 Playing for Love or Money

It is fashionable for the amateur *administrators* who run international sporting events to complain that

sportsmanship is a thing of the past and to *put the blame for everything wrong with sport on the growth of professionalism.*
5 They claim that when the modern Olympic Games began athletes felt that it was sufficient reward for them to compete. *They are horrified that* some *athletes* today regard running as work and *expect to be paid for what they do.*

The truth is that such high ideals were always an
10 aspiration and never had much to do with reality. The Olympic Games of 1900 and 1904 were tied up with business, because they were organised as a secondary attraction to international trade fairs. It was a frequent occurrence for athletes to be disqualified for breaking the
15 rules and on one occasion the losing team in the Olympic football final walked off the field and refused to go on with the game.

The love of amateurism and the belief that *what is important is how you behave on the field, not whether you win or*
20 *lose,* comes from a time when the only people who played games seriously did not need to earn their living. Even then, it was common for rich men and universities in some countries to subsidise 'amateurs' by paying their bills or tuition fees.

25 Whatever the idealists may say, it is obvious that *what matters to the public is success.* Even the organisers of the Olympic Games admit this. Whoever comes first wins a gold medal but anyone who comes fourth gets nothing. What the administrators sometimes ignore is that anyone
30 who wants to become an Olympic champion must do without spare time and possibly break off his studies. It is not surprising that athletes want some tangible reward.

The fact that sport is becoming less entertaining is more important than the question of amateurism. The
35 reason for this is that it is often easier for a team to break down another team's resistance by defensive tactics than to break through and score themselves. *In international matches,* prestige is so important that *the only thing that matters is to avoid being beaten.* In view of the fact
40 that sport will become more necessary to society in the future as entertainment, because people will have more spare time to fill, it might be better for administrators to do away with amateurism altogether and concentrate on

improving the standards of play and facilities for players
45 and spectators alike.

A Comprehension

Which of the following statements is correct in the context
of the passage?

(1) Most athletes who took part in early Olympic
Games (a) broke the rules (b) did not expect to be
paid (c) were subsidised by business interests.

(2) The administrators' love of amateurism results from
the fact that they (a) are out of date (b) are rich
(c) have played games seriously themselves.

(3) Administrators (a) do not care that athletes may
not be able to pay for their studies (b) do not know
that athletes must spend their spare time training
(c) prefer to overlook the fact that athletic success
may demand sacrifices.

(4) Sport is less entertaining than it used to be because
(a) defensive tactics are frequently successful (b) it
is played by professionals (c) there are too many
international matches.

(5) The social importance of sport in the future will
increase because (a) administrators will do away
with amateurism (b) people will need to be entertained more frequently (c) standards of play will be
improved.

B Words

Choose the word or phrase from the alternative given
which is closest in meaning to the words in italics in the
context of the passage.

(1) *Run* (1.2) (a) organise (b) take part in (c) undertake.
(2) *Regard* (1.8) (a) look at (b) look on (c) look over.
(3) *Break off* (1.31) abandon (b) give up (c) interrupt.
(4) *Beaten* (1.39) (a) defeated (b) earned (c) won.
(5) *Do away with* (1.42) (a) abolish (b) destroy (c) kill.

(6) *Altogether* (1.43) (a) all together (b) completely (c) on the whole.

(7) *Standards* (1.45) (a) degrees (b) levels (c) marks.

(8) *Alike* (1.46) (a) as well (b) equally (c) similar.

C Patterns

In each case, reproduce the pattern as indicated, substituting the words given and taking care to form the verbs correctly. Change or put in articles, possessives, prepositions where necessary.

(1a) *What matters to the public is success*
   (a) interest/audience/good acting.
   (b) attract/spectators/constant action.
   (c) upset/administrators/professionalism.

(1b) *Athletes expect to be paid for what they do*
   (a) People/ought/interested in/do.
   (b) No one/like/taxed on/earn.
   (c) The audience/want/entertained by/see.

(1c) *In international matches, the only thing that matters is to avoid being beaten.* Rewrite the sentences in (1a), substituting '*the only thing that*' for *what*.

(1d) *Administrators put the blame for everything (that is) wrong with sport on the growth of professionalism.* Rewrite the sentences in (1b), substituting *everything* for *what*.

(2) *They are horrified that athletes expect to be paid.*
   What horrifies them is that athletes expect to be paid.
   The second sentence has the same meaning as the first but is more emphatic. Change the following sentences in the same way.
   (a) They are surprised that amateurs demand expenses.
   (b) We are pleased that the children enjoy the games.
   (c) He is annoyed that the workers want overtime payment for Sunday work.

(3) *What is important is how you behave on the field, not whether you win or lose.*
- (a) how you do the job/whether you finish it quickly.
- (b) when the train arrives/where it stops.
- (c) how fast the machine works/how much it costs.

D   Whoever and Whatever

Whoever sometimes means 'the one who' or 'anyone who'. *Whoever comes first wins a gold medal but anyone who comes fourth gets nothing.* Rewrite the following sentences, substituting *anyone who* for *whoever*.
- (a) Whoever guesses the contents of the parcel will get a prize.
- (b) Whoever thinks that there are real amateurs left in international sport is naïve.
- (c) Whoever comes late will be punished.

(2) *Whoever* can also mean 'it doesn't matter who' or 'I don't care who'
I'm not going to let him in, whoever he is
Rewrite the following sentences, substituting *whoever* for the words in italic type.
- (a) You can wait in the queue like everyone else, *I don't care who you are.*
- (b) *It doesn't matter who* the fellow was, he was driving too fast.
- (c) She'll have to come back tomorrow, *I don't care who* she is.

(3) *Whatever* is used in the same way to mean 'it doesn't matter what' or 'I don't care what'.
Whatever the idealists may say, it is obvious that what matters to the public is success. Substitute *whatever* for the words in italic type in the following sentences.
- (a) *I don't care what* the administrators believe, amateurs break the rules, as well as professionals.
- (b) Do what you think is right, *it doesn't matter what* they say.
- (c) I am too wide awake to go to bed yet, *it doesn't matter what* the time is.

E   'For' and 'That' in Impersonal Constructions

It is fashionable for amateur administrators to complain that sportsmanship is a thing of the past.
It is obvious that what matters to the public is success.
Both constructions are frequently found after 'it is' + adjective. In some cases, an adjective may be followed by either, but usually we prefer one or the other. Repeat the pattern, substituting the words given.

(1) *It is common for rich men to subsidise 'amateurs'*
    (a)   necessary/athletes/train consistently.
    (b)   fashionable/administrators/criticise professionalism.
    (c)   easy/teams/play defensively.
    (d)   difficult/sportsmen/continue their studies.
    (e)   expensive/amateurs/travel to events.
    (f)   unhealthy/people/have no spare time.
    (g)   dangerous/children/play in the street.
    (h)   boring/spectators/watch international matches.

(2) *It is (not) surprising that athletes want some tangible reward*
    (a)   incredible/administrators live in the past.
    (b)   curious/some 'amateur' sportsmen earn a lot of money.
    (c)   probable/amateurism will eventually disappear.
    (d)   true/the Olympic ideal is still an aspiration.
    (e)   likely/sporting facilities will improve in the future.
    (f)   certain/my brother will be fit to run.
    (g)   lucky/the referee didn't see the foul.
    (h)   clear/the game will have to be put off.

F   Phrasal Verbs – Do

Complete the sentences with one of the following prepositions – *away with, up* (2), *with, without.*

(1)   Anyone who wants to become an Olympic champion must do .... spare time.

(2) The high ideals of the Olympic movement have never had much to do .... reality.

(3) It might be better for administrators to do .... amateurism altogether.

(4) Would you help me to do .... this parcel?

(5) We are going to have the living-room done .....

G Phrasal Verbs – Break

Complete the sentences with one of the following pre-positions – *away from, down* (4), *in, off* (2), *out, through, up.*

(1) It would be a pity if you had to break .... your studies.

(2) It is often easier for a team to break .... another team's resistance by defensive action than to break .... and score themselves.

(3) The British football association broke .... the international federation because they couldn't agree about amateurism.

(4) My car broke .... so I had to walk.

(5) The Second World War broke .... in 1939.

(6) The meeting broke .... and everyone went home.

(7) The burglar broke .... and stole the stamp collection.

(8) Carbon dioxide can be broken .... into oxygen and carbon.

(9) She broke .... when she heard the terrible news.

(10) He broke .... his engagement the day before the wedding.

H Composition

(1) Describe what is meant by the word 'amateur' in the United States, the Soviet Union and your own country.

(2) Say what you think will be the rôle of sport in society in the future.

(3) Do you think international sporting competitions encourage friendship between different countries?

PROGRESS TEST

Complete the sentences, using one word in each space.

(1) .... irritates professionals is that amateurs are often paid for .... they do.

(2) .... the tax office say, it is unreasonable for me to pay taxes on .... I earn.

(3) .... pleases me .... that the children enjoy the games.

(4) .... guesses the contents of the parcel will get a prize.

(5) You can wait in the queue .... everyone else, ... you are.

(6) .... the idealists say, it is obvious that .... matters .... the public is success.

(7) I'm afraid we've run out of butter and the shops are shut. You'll have to do .....

(8) George has had the living room done .....

(9) There was nothing more to say so the meeting broke .....

(10) We have broken .... our engagement.

26 Flying Backwards and Forwards

Air travel is such an everyday experience these days that we are not surprised when we read about a politician having talks with the Japanese Prime Minister one day, attending a conference in Australia the following morning
5   and having to be off at midday to sign a trade agreement in Bangkok. But frequent long-distance flying can be so tiring that the traveller begins to feel his brain is in one country, his digestion in another and his powers of concentration nowhere – in short, he hardly knows where
10 he is.

The fatigue we normally experience after a long

journey is accentuated when we fly from east to west or vice versa because we cross time zones. Air travel is so quick nowadays that we can leave London after breakfast
15 and be in New York in eight hours, yet what really disturbs us most is that when we arrive it is only lunch time but we have already had lunch on the plane and are expecting dinner.

Doctors say that since air travellers are in no condition to
20 *work after crossing a number of time zones, they should go straight to bed on arrival.* Airline pilots, in fact, whose experience is so obviously relevant that it ought to serve as a guide, often live by their own watches, ignoring local time, and have breakfast at midnight if necessary. *They*
25 *have far less reason to worry about their health than executives because they are used to flying* and are physically fit.

Business men who go on long-distance flights, however, are usually out for promotion and flattered to have been chosen because it adds to their status and prestige in the
30 firm. They are lucky if the company is enlightened enough to insist on them taking the doctor's advice and resting for a day before working. Sometimes *the managing director is such an energetic character that he expects everyone to be as fit as he is.* As he has never felt any ill effects after
35 flying himself, *the schedule he lays down is so exacting that the employee is too exhausted to carry it out satisfactorily.* He must either go straight to an important meeting as soon as his plane touches down or else return as soon as the meeting is over to report to his boss. Dynamic tycoons of
40 this type often do not realise how disastrous this policy may be for the man's health and the company's reputation.

A Comprehension

Which of the following statements is correct in the context of the passage?

(1) (a) We experience fatigue on flights only when we cross time zones
(b) we experience fatigue on a long flight only when we fly towards the west

    (c) crossing time zones increases the fatigue we experience on a flight.

(2) After long-distance flights pilots (a) always go straight to bed (b) find it wisest to take no notice of local time (c) have breakfast.

(3) Businessmen often take no notice of doctors' advice because they are (a) physically fit (b) keen to impress people (c) enlightened.

(4) If a managing director is energetic he frequently (a) refuses to allow his employees to lie down (b) makes his employees attend classes to keep fit (c) expects too much of his employees.

(5) The policy adopted by dynamic tycoons is likely to be disastrous for the company's reputation because their employees (a) are obviously unkindly treated (b) are not given time to make friends on meetings abroad (c) may make serious mistakes because of tiredness.

B Words

Choose the word or phrase from the alternatives given which is closest in meaning to the words in italics in the context of the passage.

(1) *Attending* (1.4) (a) listening to (b) being present at (c) assisting at.

(2) *The following* (1.4) (a) the other (b) the next (c) the successive.

(3) *Tiring* (1.7) (a) exhausting (b) boring (c) weary.

(4) *Ignoring* (1.23) (a) taking no notice of (b) not knowing (c) forgetting.

(5) *Out for* (1.28) (a) abroad because of (b) unable to get (c) keen to obtain.

(6) *Enlightened* (1.30) (a) intelligent (b) spiritual (c) illuminated.

(7) *Resting* (1.32) (a) remaining (b) relaxing (c) staying.

(8) *Exacting* (1.35) (a) precise (b) accurate (c) demanding.

C   Patterns

(1) *Doctors say that since air travellers are in no condition to work after crossing a number of time zones, they should go straight to bed on arrival.*

This sentence could be rewritten 'Doctors say that air travellers should go straight to bed on arrival *because* they are in no condition to work after crossing a number of time zones'. It would also be possible to substitute *as* for *since* in the first sentence without changing the meaning.

Rewrite the following sentences, using *because* in the sentence instead of *as* or *since* and putting the clause second in the sentence instead of first.

(a) Since he was in no condition to work, the doctor told him to rest.

(b) As he has never felt any ill effects after flying himself, he is surprised when his employees complain.

(c) Since I had missed the last bus home, my friend put me up for the night.

(d) As he couldn't speak English, he didn't understand me.

(e) Since he is very energetic himself, he expects his employees to work hard.

(2) *They have far less reason to worry about their health than executives because they are used to flying.* This sentence could be rewritten '*As/Since* they are used to flying, they have far less reason to worry about their health than executives'. Rewrite the following sentences, using *as* or *since* in place of *because* and putting the clause first in the sentence instead of second.

(a) Businessmen usually like flying because it adds to their status and prestige.

(b) He couldn't answer her letter because she had forgotten to write her address at the top.

(c) The manager called the police because the man refused to pay his bill.

(d) I don't know what decisions were taken at the conference because our representative hasn't reported to me yet.

G

(e) They are going on strike because they have not been paid for the work they have done.

(3) *The managing director is such an energetic character that he expects everyone to be as fit as he is.*

We could express the meaning of this sentence differently by saying 'The managing director is *so* energetic that he expects everyone to be as fit as he is'. Convert the following sentences to the form of the second by using *so*.

(a) It was such a tiring journey that I felt exhausted when we landed. (Begin 'The journey . . . .)

(b) It is such a fast train that it gets to London in forty minutes.

(c) They were such nice people at the hotel that it was a pleasure to meet them.

(d) It was such a long conference that I was glad when it was over.

(4) *The schedule he lays down is so exacting that the employee is too exhausted to carry it out satisfactorily.* This sentence could be rewritten – *He lays down* such *an exacting schedule that the employee is too exhausted to carry it out satisfactorily.*

Convert the following sentences to the form of the second by using *such*.

(a) The flight was so long that we had three meals on board the plane. (Begin 'It was such . . . .)

(b) The company is so enlightened that it always takes care of its employees' health.

(c) The book was so boring that I couldn't finish it.

(d) The policy was so disastrous that it ruined the company's reputation.

(e) The boxes were so large that we could not send them by air.

D Be + Preposition

Substitute the present tense of the verb *Be* with one of the following prepositions for the phrases in italics: *back, off* (2), *on, out, out for, out of, over, up* (2), *up to.*

(1) Businessmen who *are keen to get* promotion are flattered to be chosen for a long distance flight.

(2) I *am starting my flight* to Bangkok on the 2 o'clock plane.

(3) I must return to England as soon as the meeting *has finished*.

(4) It has been raining so hard that this afternoon's game *has been cancelled*.

(5) He's *not at home* at the moment. I'll let you know as soon as he *returns*.

(6) If I *haven't gone to bed* when you arrive home, I'll make you some coffee.

(7) What's *happening*? You look upset.

(8) We *haven't any* sugar *left*. I forgot to buy some.

(9) What film *is being shown* at the Ritz this week?

(10) Those children *are* always *doing* something *mischievous*.

E   Composition

(1) Explain the effects that long-distance flights can have on businessmen and politicians.

(2) Your firm has received a letter complaining that an order has not been delivered. Reply, giving reasons for the delay and promising delivery soon.

PROGRESS TEST

Link the sentences together, using the words in brackets.

(1) He had to catch a plane as soon as the conference ended. It wasn't surprising that he didn't have time to write a report. (as)

(2) He left home early. He was afraid of missing the plane. (because)

(3) I don't know what happened at the meeting. I can't be expected to comment on it. (since)

(4) You must go straight to the boss's office. He is waiting for your report. (because)

(5) Long plane journeys are often very tiring. People feel exhausted when they land. (so . . . that)

(6) The flight tickets were very expensive. Nobody wanted to pay for them. (so . . . that)

(7) He is a very energetic man. He never seems to get tired. (such . . . that)

(8) He had a very violent temper. People were afraid of him. (such . . . that)
(9) The pilot was very young. Nobody trusted him. (so . . that)
(10) It was a very important meeting. He felt that he had to attend it. (such . . . that)

27 Gold is the Devil

One day in 1848 a carpenter named Marshall, who worked in a saw mill on the American River in California, made a remarkable discovery. He noticed some bright yellow particles in the water, bent down to pick them up and

5   took them to his partner, a Mr Sutter. This was the beginning of the Californian Gold Rush. Sutter was a Swiss who had come to America some years earlier to make his fortune. The Governor of California had given him permission to found a settlement in the Sacramento

10 Valley and his determination and energy had made him rich. *He had built the mill* in partnership with Marshall *in order to make use of the abundant natural resources of his land.*
  Sutter realized the importance of the discovery and *decided to file a claim so that his right to the gold would be*

15 *established.* So *he sent* a man named *Bennet to San Francisco to see the Governor. He warned Bennet not to tell anyone in case people came to the valley before his claim was recognised.* Bennet could not keep the secret but the people of San Francisco did not believe him at first. Then the editor of

20 a weekly newspaper there, *Sam Brannan, went to Sutter's mill to make a report.* When he came back he ran through the streets of the town shouting 'Gold! Gold!' Within a month almost the entire population, then only 800 people, had gone to look for the precious metal. Soldiers

25 deserted the army, sailors left their ships and *men gave up their jobs so as not to miss the chance of becoming rich.*
  The news spread across America to Europe and thousands of people joined in the search. Those who went by

30

ship had to sail round Cape Horn to reach California but some chose the overland route across America and *wagon trains were formed for travellers to make the journey.* Even then there were some who were prepared to cross the terrible desert of Death Valley in order to reach the gold a few days before the rest.

35

The Gold Rush proved a disaster for Sutter himself. For years *he tried to evict the prospectors* from his property *so that his family might enjoy the wealth of his land,* but his business was ruined. The prospectors did a great deal of damage, and killed one of his sons, and at the end of his

40

life he was a poor man who continually stopped people in the street to tell them that Gold is the Devil.

A Comprehension

Which of the following statements is correct in the context of the passage?

(1) Sutter (a) had become rich by selling land granted to him by the Governor (b) had come to America to look for gold (c) had made a fortune by developing the natural resources of the Sacramento Valley.

(2) Sutter sent Bennet to San Francisco (a) to ask the Governor for permission to found a settlement (b) to make sure that any gold found on his land would belong to him (c) to prevent people from coming to the Sacramento Valley.

(3) The people of San Francisco (a) set out for the valley as soon as Bennet told them about the gold (b) did not believe the story until they read it in the newspaper (c) were convinced about the gold when one of the citizens confirmed Bennet's story.

(4) Wagon trains were formed so that (a) groups of people could cross the American continent together (b) none of the travellers would get lost (c) travellers could cross Death Valley safely.

(5) Sutter was ruined because the prospectors (a) took all the gold from his land (b) prevented him from making use of his property (c) killed one of his sons.

B Words

Choose the word or phrase from the alternatives given which is closest in meaning to the words in italics in the context of the passage.

(1) *Took* (1.5) (a) carried (b) brought (c) fetched
(2) *Partner* (1.5) (a) colleague (b) business associate (c) shareholder
(3) *Abundant natural resources* (1.12) (a) trees growing in profusion (b) rich soil (c) mineral wealth
(4) *His claim was recognised* (1.17) (a) his attempt to obtain the gold was noticed (b) his mine was seen (c) his right to the gold was officially confirmed
(5) *Precious* (1.24) (a) expensive (b) very valuable (c) worthy
(6) *Prepared* (1.32) (a) made ready (b) willing (c) trained
(7) *The rest* (1.34) (a) the others (b) the remains (c) the relaxation
(8) *Proved* (1.35) (a) tested (b) turned out to be (c) demonstrated

C Patterns

Study the pattern in italic type in each case and then reproduce it, substituting the words given and taking care to form the verbs correctly. Change or put in articles, possessives, prepositions where necessary.

(1) *Sam Brannan went to Sutter's mill to make a report*
 (a) Sutter/emigrate/America/make his fortune
 (b) Many people/sail/Cape Horn/reach California
 (c) The prospectors/form/wagon trains/defend themselves

(2) *He* (had) *built the mill in order to make use of the abundant natural resources of his land*
 (a) Some prospectors/cross/Death Valley/reach the gold first
 (b) Some people/choose/the overland route/avoid a long voyage
 (c) He/establish/a settlement/develop the valley

(3) *He sent Bennet to San Francisco to see the Governor*
  (a) I/send/him/post office/buy some stamps
  (b) He/buy/her/a present/make her happy
  (c) Sutter/tell/them/his life story/prove his statement

(4) *Men gave up their jobs so as not to miss the chance of becoming rich*
  (a) They/go/overland/waste time
  (b) I/turn off/the television/wake the baby
  (c) He/agree with/them/ cause an argument

(5) *Wagon trains were formed for travellers to make the journey*
  (a) The settlement/establish/immigrants/begin a new life
  (b) The money/leave/sick people/benefit from it
  (c) The meeting/held/the citizens/express their views

(6) *Sutter decided to file a claim so that his right* (to the gold) *would be established*
  (a) He/give her an injection/pain/bearable
  (b) We/open a bank account/money/safe
  (c) They/work all night/job/finished

(7) *He tried to evict the prospectors so that his family might enjoy the wealth of his land*
  (a) Sutter/get in touch with/the Governor/the Governor/confirm his right to the gold
  (b) People/form/wagon trains/the prospectors/travel more safely
  (c) He/call/a meeting/everyone/discuss the matter openly

D In Case

He warned Bennet not to tell anyone in case people came to the valley before his claim was recognised
In this sentence, *In case* has the meaning 'because (he was afraid that) people might come'. Use it, followed by the Past Simple tense, to replace the words in italics in the following sentences.
  (1) Men left their jobs *because they were afraid* people

might take all the gold before they arrived at the mill.

(2) I gave him a map *because I thought* he *might not know* the way to my house.

(3) He took an umbrella with him *because he thought* it *might rain*.

(4) We put up a notice *because we were afraid* people *might not know* where the meeting was being held.

(5) He insured his car *because he was afraid* he *might have* an accident.

E Do and Make

Complete the following sentences, choosing which of these two verbs is correct and using the correct form.

(1) Marshall .... a remarkable discovery on the American River.

(2) Many of the settlers preferred to .... the dangerous overland journey to California instead of .... the long voyage round Cape Horn.

(3) Sutter went to America to .... his fortune.

(4) He .... good business at first and .... a lot of money.

(5) The prospectors .... a great deal of damage to his property.

(6) He built the mill to .... use of the resources of his land.

(7) Sutter did not .... the prospectors welcome.

(8) The settlers frequently .... war on the Indians.

(9) The Indians often .... attacks on the wagon trains.

(10) Sutter .... a complaint to the Governor when the prospectors arrived but it didn't .... him any good.

(11) The Governor knew they had .... wrong but by the time he had .... his enquiries, the men had .... their escape.

(12) I have .... the repairs and I think you will find that I have .... a good job of them.

(13) .... your homework and .... sure that you don't .... many mistakes.

(14) Instead of .... his own work he .... trouble by .... work for everyone else.

F   Composition

(1) Explain what Sutter tried to do to keep the gold in the Sacramento Valley for himself and his family and how the Californian Gold Rush took place and developed.

(2) Explain the purpose and development of (a) a new law (b) a new transport or communication system, or (c) an invention in your country or elsewhere.

(3) You were responsible for organising (a) a wedding reception (b) a dinner in honour of an important visitor or (c) a sporting competition between teams from different countries. Say what plans you made and why and what instructions you gave.

PROGRESS TEST

Link the sentences together, using the words in brackets where required. Leave out unnecessary words where the construction is different.

(1) I went to the station. I intended to see my friend off.

(2) The prospectors travelled together in wagon trains. They wanted to defend themselves against Indian attacks. (in order to)

(3) The prospectors travelled together in wagon trains. They were afraid that Indians might attack them. (in case)

(4) I sent him to the greengrocer's. I wanted him to buy some oranges.

(5) I closed the door quietly. I didn't want to wake the baby. (so as not to)

(6) I closed the door quietly. I was afraid that I might wake the baby. (in case)

(7) Facilities were provided. Their purpose was to enable students to do research work. (for students to)

(8) He left some money in his will. He intended that his family would be provided for. (so that)

(9) He left her a message. He intended that she would know where to find him. (so that)

(10) The police put up pictures of the wanted man. They hoped that he might be recognized and arrested. (so that)

28 Killing without Meaning To

Over a hundred years ago, when Melville wrote his famous novel 'Moby Dick', hunting whales was a dangerous and sometimes fatal business. Now, *in spite of their size, whales are no longer an even match for men* using helicopters, radar and explosive harpoons. As a result, some species, such as the giant blue whale, are on the verge of becoming extinct. Although some countries gave up whaling several years ago, there was no international agreement forbidding it until recently, in spite of the fact that alternatives to the whale products used in oils, cosmetics and candles were already in existence.

The whale is not the only species fighting for survival. In the United States alone, conservationists have estimated that over a hundred kinds of animals, fish and birds will disappear before the end of the century unless action is taken to protect them. *Although governments* in many countries *have done a great deal* to control hunting and fishing for sport and have set up game reserves and bird sanctuaries where the species can breed safely in their natural surroundings, *the number in danger is still increasing.*

Rare animals useful to the fashion industry *are still hunted, even though we can now imitate their skins* and furs with other products. Nevertheless, some progress is being made. In certain regiments of the British army soldiers used to wear leopard skins but now these are manufactured from plastics. In New York the sale of animal skins and furs has been forbidden and this may have preserved the American alligator from extinction, as well as other animals hunted in Africa.

The greatest problem for conservationists is that *while we can make laws* to protect certain species *we are frequently incapable of controlling the environment* in which they live and breed. *In spite of taking action to prevent it, we may contaminate rivers* and make the fish sterile. *However good our intentions are* in destroying the insects and vermin that eat our crops, at the same time *we deprive the birds* that live on them *of food.* Man has not yet learnt how to deal with the balance of

nature and *whatever he does, he is bound to alter it* without realizing it. But even though it may not be possible to
40 save every endangered species from extinction, we should be able to protect the majority by becoming aware of their plight before it is too late.

A Comprehension

Which one of the following statements is correct in the context of the passage?

(1) Hunting whales (a) has always been dangerous (b) is only dangerous if the whales are very large (c) is not very dangerous nowadays.

(2) (a) Only a few countries still engage in whaling (b) There is no international agreement forbidding whaling (c) Whaling has now been stopped by international agreement.

(3) (a) Governments are not conscious of the dangers threatening certain species (b) In spite of government action, the number of species in danger of extinction is increasing (c) Government action has reduced the number of species in danger of extinction.

(4) The greatest problem conservationists face is that (a) Governments are not aware of the threat to wild life (b) People go on hunting species protected by law (c) We cannot help affecting the natural environment, whatever we do.

(5) (a) It is wrong to destroy insects and vermin (b) We are now able to destroy the birds that eat our crops as well as insects and vermin (c) We destroy birds without meaning to.

B Words

Choose the word or phrase from the alternatives given which is closest in meaning to the word in italics in the context of the passage.

(1) *Are no longer an even match for* (1.4) (a) do not fight

fairly any more against (b) cannot now fight on equal terms with (c) are still on unequal terms with.
(2) *Such as* (1.5) (a) so like (b) like (c) alike.
(3) *In existence* (1.11) (a) in stock (b) available (c) living
(4) *Estimated* (1.13) (a) calculated (b) valued (c) decided
(5) *Control* (1.17) (a) prevent (b) prohibit (c) limit
(6) *Game reserves* (1.18) (a) supplies of animals for hunting (b) places where animals are protected from hunters (c) sports grounds
(7) *Preserved* (1.27) (a) saved (b) prevented (c) avoided
(8) *Bound to* (1.38) (a) tied to (b) certain to (c) obliged to

C   Patterns

Study the patterns and reproduce them, substituting the words given. Change or put in articles, possessives, prepositions, where necessary and make sure that the verbs are in the correct tense.

(1) *Although governments have done a great deal, the number* (of species) *in danger is still increasing*
   (a) workers/make good progress/the work remaining/enormous
   (b) weather forecast/promise sunshine/the temperature outside/falling
   (c) company/pay that bill/the money outstanding/considerable

(2) *Rare animals are still hunted, even though we can now imitate their skins* (with other products)
   (a) Leopard skins/worn/make them from plastics
   (b) Hunting/allowed/enjoy other sporting facilities
   (c) Genuine fur coats/bought/make them synthetically

(3) *Whatever he does, man is bound to alter the environment*
   (a) you say/he/sure/disagree with you
   (b) we intend/we/certain/destroy other species
   (c) they earn/they/likely/demand a rise

(4) *However good our intentions are, we deprive the birds of food*
   (a) intelligent a man is/he needs/help of machines
   (b) beautiful a woman is/she prefers/aid of cosmetics
   (c) convincing an argument is/it needs/support of evidence

(5) *While we can make laws* (to protect certain species) *we are frequently incapable of controlling the environment*
   (a) man/destroy species/he/often/preserving them
   (b) women/buy imitation fur coats/they/sometimes/resisting real ones
   (c) the children/understand numbers/they/frequently/reading words

D In Spite Of

In spite of is used with the same meaning as *although* but is followed by a noun or gerund. In each of the following sentences, replace *in spite of* by *although*, and instead of the noun or gerund which follows, use a verb in the same tense as the verb in the second part of the sentence, together with an appropriate adjective.

(1) *In spite of their size, whales are no longer an even match for men*
   Although they are very large, whales are no longer an even match for men
   (a) In spite of their rarity, these animals are still hunted.
   (b) In spite of his intelligence, he failed the examination.
   (c) In spite of his strength, he couldn't lift the weight.
   (d) In spite of its speed, the horse didn't win the race.
   (e) In spite of his bad temper, she still loves him.

(2) *In spite of taking action to prevent it, we may contaminate rivers*
   Although we may take action to prevent it, we may contaminate rivers
   (a) In spite of failing to save every endangered

species, we may preserve the majority from extinction.

(b) In spite of living in the city, he prefers the country.

(c) In spite of arriving late at the station, he still caught the train.

(d) In spite of working all night, he didn't finish the job.

(e) In spite of training hard for the race, he was beaten.

E   Participles as Alternatives to a Relative Clause

We frequently leave out a defining relative clause using 'who' or 'that' as subject of the verb and substitute the present participle.

(1) *The whale is not the only species* (that is) *fighting for survival*

Rewrite the following sentences, changing the part in italic type to a present participle.

(a) The train *that is standing* at Platform 1 will leave in ten minutes.

(b) Although we don't mean to, we deprive the birds *that live* on these insects of food.

(c) Until recently, there was no international agreement *that forbade* whaling.

(d) Anyone *who answers* the questions correctly will receive a prize.

(e) People *who live* on the slopes of active volcanoes know that they may erupt at any moment.

In the same way, we often leave out the relative part of a defining relative clause where 'who' or 'that' is the subject of a passive verb, employing the past participle alone.

(2) *This may have preserved the American alligator from extinction, as well as other animals* (that are) *hunted in Africa*

Rewrite the following sentences, leaving out the words in italic type.

    (a) The letters *that were* posted last week must have arrived by now.

    (b) The inspector *who had been* sent to investigate the robbery soon realised that Minty Miller was responsible.

    (c) The facilities *that are* provided by the Government are inadequate.

    (d) The work *that has been* done so far does not indicate a quick solution to the problem.

    (e) The insecticides *that are* used on the crops often kill birds as well.

F   Composition

    (1) Explain why it is difficult for governments to save species in danger of extinction, in spite of the action they are taking.

    (2) Why is it difficult to control pollution in cities? Explain the problems facing governments and city authorities, using a city in your own country as an example.

PROGRESS TEST
Link the sentences together, using the words in brackets. Leave out unnecessary words where the construction is different.

    (1) Some countries gave up whaling several years ago. But there was no international agreement forbidding it until recently. (although)

    (2) Whales are very large. But they are no match for men with explosive harpoons. (although)

    (3) She still wanted to marry him. It didn't matter to her that he had lost all his money. (even though)

    (4) We understand the problem. But we cannot resolve it. (even though)

    (5) We can make laws. We cannot always enforce them. (While)

    (6) It doesn't matter what he does. She always forgives him. (whatever)

(7) It doesn't matter that you are very busy. You have to stop work occasionally to eat. (However)

(8) It won't matter if the situation becomes very serious. I'll still support you. (However)

Section Four

Composition

29 Personal Letters

(1) *Asking for Help and Advice*

> Calle Amigo 150,
> Barcelona – 32,
> Spain.
> 26th June, 1973

Dear Sheila,

I've just had some marvellous news. I've passed my final examinations at the university and my father was so pleased (or maybe surprised) that he offered to pay for
5 a holiday abroad. I'd like to come to England for a month or so to improve my English and naturally to see you again.

I wonder if you could do me a favour. As I've left it too late to enrol at the language school where I studied last
10 year, could you find out whether there are any summer courses in your area? What I'm really looking for is an advanced course, three or four hours a day, leaving the afternoons free. *I imagine you'll be on vacation yourself* from the university so perhaps we could go out and see some
15 of the places we didn't have time to visit last year.

I'd be grateful if you'd let me know as soon as possible *about the courses* and also find out if the school could fix up a room for me. I know how generous your parents are – *I enjoyed myself so much when I stayed with you last year –*
20 so I must say in advance that I wouldn't dream of putting them to any trouble.

> Please give them my kindest regards.
> Sincerely,
> Carlos

(2) *Thanking Someone for a Letter and Answering It*

> 28 Woodside Avenue,
> Southwich,
> Lincolnshire, England.
> 2nd July, 1973

Dear Carlos,

I was so glad to have your letter and know that *we'll see*

each other again quite soon. I've made enquiries locally and discovered that there's a month's advanced course
5   at the Polytechnic here beginning on July 15th. It looks as if it's just what you want. I'm enclosing the enrolment forms so that you can post them off straightaway.

The Polytechnic would find accommodation for you but that seems a pity when we're just round the corner.
10 I've spoken to Mother and Father about it and they'd be very happy to have you here. Don't feel shy about accepting. There's a spare room quite big enough for you to study in. Of course, *Mother wouldn't hear of accepting anything for your stay* but if your pride is involved I expect
15 you could come to an arrangement with her about meals.

We look forward to having you with us again. Let me know how and when you are coming so that I can meet you.

> Remember me to your parents.
> Love,
> Sheila

A   Polite and 'Hidden' Conditionals

(1) *I'd be grateful if you'd let me know about the courses*
We frequently use a double conditional pattern (I *would* be grateful if you *would* . . .) when we are asking someone for help in a polite way. Repeat the pattern, substituting the words provided.
   (a) glad/reply as soon as possible
   (b) happy/suggest it to him
   (c) obliged/pay attention to what I'm saying

(2) *I wonder if you could do me a favour*
This pattern with *could* is another polite way of asking for help. Repeat it, substituting the words provided.
   (a) give me some advice
   (b) help me with my homework
   (c) solve this problem for me

(3) *Mother wouldn't hear of accepting anything for your stay*
This is a hidden' conditional because it uses *would* without the other half of the sentence we are used to. It implies that the sentence could be completed 'if you offered it'

or 'whatever you offered'. Repeat the pattern, using the words provided. Make sure that the verbs are in the correct form.

    (a) I/dream of/turn down such an opportunity
    (b) I/think of/impose on your parents
    (c) I/be afraid of/speak to the boss about it

B   'Be' + adjective + 'To'

I was so glad to have your letter
Repeat the pattern in the following sentences, substituting the words provided.

    (a) We/pleased/receive/invitation
    (b) I/happy/have/news
    (c) We/delighted/get/postcard
    (d) I/sorry/hear about/illness
    (e) We/excited/learn of/success

C Self and Each Other

    (1) *I enjoyed myself so much when I stayed with you last year*
Reflexive pronouns are used when the action reflects on the subject and with the verbs *enjoy* (oneself), *help* (oneself) (to) and *avail* (oneself) *of*. Complete the sentences with the correct reflexive pronoun.

    (a) You're old enough to look after . . . .
    (b) Problems don't usually solve . . . .
    (c) Like most young girls, she is fond of looking at
        . . . . in the mirror.
    (d) Don't wait to be invited. Help . . . . to a drink.
    (e) We enjoyed . . . . very much at the party.
    (f) He lives a long way from a language school so
        he's been trying to teach . . . .
    (g) Don't touch that electric cable. You'll kill . . . .
    (h) I'll be glad to avail . . . . of your kind offer.

    (2) *I'm having a holiday and I imagine you'll be on vacation yourself*
The reflexive pronouns are sometimes used for emphasis and in certain cases have a similar meaning to *too*. Com-

plete the following sentences with the correct reflexive pronoun.

   (a) The boss is going to work late so I expect we'll have to stay late at the office ....
   (b) All our friends are going to the party and of course I'm going ....
   (c) They .... offered to do it. We didn't need to ask them.
   (d) There's no need for me to tell you the way to the house. I'll come to the station .... to meet you.
   (e) She can't blame me if she doesn't like the dress. She chose it ....

(3) *We'll see each other again quite soon*
Each other (or *one another*) is used when an action or feeling is mutual.
Use it in the following sentences.

   (a) We'll never finish the job if we don't co-operate with ... .
   (b) Stop fighting, you two! You'll hurt ... .
   (c) We mustn't put Dick near Alex at the dinner. They can't bear ... .
   (d) They've quarrelled and don't speak to ... . any more.
   (e) We're sure to have a lot to tell ... . after such a long time without seeing ... .

D Composition

Here are some subjects for personal letters. Write about 120–150 words and lay out the letters in the same way as in the examples.

   (1) You have received a Christmas present from a friend. Write a letter thanking him/her for the present and briefly explaining how you spent Christmas.
   (2) You are ill and realise that you will be unable to go to dinner at a friend's house the following evening.

Write to him/her to explain and invite him/her to your own house at a later date.

(3) You would like to spend a few months in England staying with an English family. Write to a friend asking him/her to help you.

(4) You are having a party to celebrate moving into your new house (a house-warming party). Invite a friend to the party, giving him directions which will enable him/her to find the house.

(5) You are in hospital after a car accident. Write a letter to a friend thanking him/her for a present you have received and explaining how the accident happened.

(6) A member of your family is ill and you must look after him/her. Write to your employer explaining why you will have to be away from work for a few days and how soon you expect to return.

(7) You have made enquiries about a holiday abroad at various travel agencies. Write to a friend who is interested in going with you explaining what you have found out and asking for his/her opinion.

(8) You have just received a letter from a friend complaining that he/she has had no news from you for several months. Write apologising and explaining what you have been doing.

(9) A relative of yours has promised to give you a large sum of money as a reward for passing an examination. Write thanking him/her and explaining how you propose to use the gift.

(10) You are holding a children's party for your son or daughter, who wants to invite several children from school but is too young to write. Write a letter to the parents of one of the children, explaining what sort of party it is going to be and giving them directions to your house.

30 More Formal Letters

(1) *Applying for a Job*

Rue des Pins 30,
Cannes 34, France.
15th April, 1973

Dear Sirs,

I have just seen your advertisement in the "Sunday Times" of 12th April for a guide to accompany parties of British tourists in the south of France during the summer months. I am therefore enclosing a curriculum vitae, together with references from two companies I have worked for.

As you can see, I was born and brought up in Nice and therefore know the French Riviera well. I studied modern languages at school and afterwards went to England, where I obtained the Cambridge Lower Certificate two years ago. Since then I have worked as a free-lance translator and interpreter. I have often been asked to act as a guide to groups of English-speaking businessmen attending conferences in different towns on the Riviera and am confident that I would be suitable for the kind of work you are advertising.

If you would like any further information, I would be very pleased to supply it. Looking forward to hearing from you,

Yours faithfully,
Josiane Duval

Riviera Tours Ltd.,
18 Hastings Road,
Manchester 16 3BG,
England
Enc: 3

(2) *Giving a Reference*

87 Ribblesdale St.,
Preston,
Lancs.
24/11/1973

Dear Sir,

My friend Janet Simpson has applied for a post as a

secretary with your firm and I understand that you
would like a character reference in support of her
5   application.

I have known Janet for ten years. We were at school
together and later attended the Preston Secretarial
College. Apart from that, I frequently saw Janet socially
because we were both members of the same youth
10   club. For the past year and a half we have been working
in the Accounts Department at Mather and Rivers
(Engineering) Limited.

Janet is an honest, straightforward person with a
cheerful personality who gets on well with people from
15   all walks of life. She has always been enthusiastic about
her work and is quick to adapt herself to circumstances.
At the same time, she is punctual, reliable and always
takes great care of her appearance.

I am sure that she would be suitable for the post she
20   has applied for and have no hesitation in recommending
her to you.

Yours faithfully,
Agnes Cartwright

The Personnel Officer,
Brearley and Walker Ltd.,
37 Half Moon Lane,
Preston,
Lancs.

(3) *Making a Complaint*

33 Holmford Court,
Carlton St.,
Birmingham 42 7TF,
June 6, 1973

Dear Sir,

I am writing to you to express my dissatisfaction with
the service offered by your company on a recent flight
from Gatwick to Palma de Mallorca (16/5/1973, Flight
5   QYZ 123).

In the first place, we found on arrival at the airport
that flights were subject to delay. It was impossible to
make out from the loudspeaker announcements whether
this would affect our own flight so we asked the girl at

10   your information desk if there was any change in the flight plan. 'We'll let you know,' she replied, without looking up from the magazine she was reading. In the event, we had to wait seven hours before our flight was called.

15   In such circumstances, most airlines offer vouchers for meals, which makes up to some extent for the inconvenience suffered, but when I enquired about lunch, I was told that no vouchers were available. 'If you want to make out a formal complaint, you are welcome to do so,' the girl said, offering me a form. I declined the form

20   but am now following her advice.

    The flight itself was uneventful. Again no information was provided and no food was served except a cup of coffee and a biscuit. The steward explained that the company never serve meals on short morning flights,

25   ignoring the fact that by this time it was 5 o'clock in the afternoon and none of the passengers had had lunch because we were afraid that the plane would take off without us. I would be interested to know what excuse you can offer for such deplorable service.

Yours faithfully,
Andrew Singleton

The Managing Director,
Courtesy Charters Ltd.,
256 Buckingham Rd.,
London W.C.5 8DW

A Phrasal Verbs – Make

Complete the sentences with one of the following prepositions – *for, out* (3), *over, up* (3), *up for, up to*

(1) 'If you want to make .... a formal complaint, you are welcome to do so,' the girl said.

(2) It was impossible to make .... from the loudspeaker announcements whether our own flight was affected.

(3) A good meal sometimes makes .... the delay to some extent when you are held up at an airport.

(4) Bad service does not make .... good relations between a company and its clients.

(5) They are not as courteous as they make ....

(6) He likes making .... stories to entertain the children.

(7) Whenever we go out, she spends half an hour making .... her face.

(8) Do you mind working late this evening? We'll make .... the time .... you next week.

(9) How many stamps do you need to make .... the set?

(10) In his will, he made .... all his property to his wife.

B Collocations (2)

Complete the sentences with one of the following – *in, on, to, with*.

(1) Thanking you .... advance for your help, I remain.

(2) A number of animals are .... danger of extinction.

(3) They are .... the verge of becoming extinct.

(4) After flying for several hours, travellers are .... no condition to take decisions.

(5) Whales are the largest mammals .... existence.

(6) The traveller begins to feel his brain is in one country, and his digestion in another – .... short, he hardly knows where he is.

(7) I have a number of complaints to make. .... the first place, we found .... arrival at the airport that flights were subject to delay.

(8) The girl told us she would let us know about the flight but .... effect we had to wait seven hours for information.

(9) Vouchers for meals make up for the inconvenience suffered .... some extent.

(10) .... regard to your letter of June 1st, we are now .... a position to complete your May order .... addition .... the order we have just received for June.

C Composition

Here are some suggestions for more formal letters. Write

about 150 words and lay out the letters in the same way as in the examples. Consult the notes if you need advice on punctuation and on beginning and ending the letters.

(1) You have seen an advertisement for a job in a newspaper. Write applying for it.

(2) A friend of yours has applied for a job. Write a reference in support of his/her application.

(3) You have bought a television/washing machine/record player/electric cooker which does not work properly. Write to the manufacturers explaining what has happened and claiming free service under the guarantee.

(4) You were badly served in a shop or restaurant or on a journey. Write complaining about the treatment you received.

(5) You would like to study at a language school in England. Write to one that has been recommended to you by a friend enquiring about the courses offered, dates when they begin, cost, accommodation and meals etc.

(6) You have been unable to obtain some English books in your own country. Write to an English publisher, asking the firm to send the books to you and enquiring about ways of paying for them.

31 Dialogue

(1) *Asking for a Loan*

TOM Good morning, Dad. Would you mind doing me a favour?

MR BRADFORD What is it, Tom?

TOM I was wondering if you could lend me five pounds.

	MR BRADFORD	That seems a lot. What do you want so much money for?
	TOM	It's Janet's birthday on Saturday and she's having a party. I'll have to get a
10		new shirt and tie.
	MR BRADFORD	But I gave you some money last week. Have you already spent it?
	TOM	No, but I need it to buy Janet's present. If I don't go, Dad, she'll never forgive
15		me, and as I'm her boy-friend, I'll have to look smart.
	MR BRADFORD	I didn't think girls worried about things like that any more. When will you pay me back?
20	TOM	As soon as I can, Dad. Next month, perhaps.
	MR BRADFORD	Next year's more likely. Oh well, here you are.

(2) *Doing Up the Sitting-room*

	ANNE	We ought to have the sitting-room done up, George. The wallpaper's beginning to peel and the paint's scratched in some places where the children have been
5		playing.
	GEORGE	Yes, it looks a bit of a mess, darling, doesn't it? I'll do it up as soon as I have a weekend free.
	ANNE	I didn't think you would have time to do
10		it yourself, George. And you always lose your temper if things go wrong. Wouldn't it be better to leave the job to someone else?
	GEORGE	Do you mean that I'm not capable of dec-
15		orating the room myself?
	ANNE	Of course not, darling, but I hate to see you working at the weekend when you're tired.
	GEORGE	Well, to tell the truth, I have had rather
20		a lot to do lately.
	ANNE	I'm glad you agree. I've enquired at the

shop in Market Street and they've quoted a very reasonable price. So I'll tell them to come round next week.

(3) *A Television Interview*

CLIVE WELLS — I am happy to welcome viewers to my programme. My guest tonight is James Stanford, who has been one of this country's finest Shakespearian actors for many years. But I believe you've never made a film, James.

5

STANFORD — In fact, I've just finished making my first, a spy picture.

WELLS — Did you find it difficult to get used to the new medium?

10

STANFORD — At first, yes. It's hard to act for a camera and a lot of technicians when one is used to a live audience. Rather like being on television, actually.

15 WELLS — What's the film about? Is it a historical spy picture?

STANFORD — No. For once I'm playing a modern part. I'm supposed to be a counter-espionage agent.

20 WELLS — Did you have to disguise yourself for the part? You must be used to wearing a false beard and so on in your Shakespearian roles.

STANFORD — Only the usual make-up. For once the audience will be able to see my real face when the film comes out.

25

WELLS — One last question, James. Why have you made this extraordinary change, from the stage to the screen and from Shakespeare to a modern spy drama?

30

STANFORD — For money, of course. Why do you think I'm here tonight?

A Reported Speech (1)

In the exercises that follow, a conversation is written in

reported speech. Write what you think the speakers actually said. Do not refer to the dialogues in the text that you have already read until you finish these exercises. You should use the account in reported speech as a guide but take the opportunity to make the conversation as realistic as possible and use short forms wherever you can.

(1) Tom asked his father if he would mind doing him a favour. When his father asked what it was, Tom said he had been wondering if he could lend him five pounds. Mr Bradford commented that that seemed a lot. He asked what Tom wanted so much money for. Tom explained that it was Janet's birthday the following Saturday and she was having a party so he would have to get a new shirt and tie. Mr Bradford said he had given Tom some money the week before. He was surprised that Tom had already spent it. Tom said that he hadn't but he needed it to buy a present for Janet. If he didn't go to the party, she would never forgive him, he added, and as he was her boy-friend, he would have to look smart. Mr Bradford said he hadn't thought girls worried about things like that any more. He asked Tom when he would pay him back. Tom replied that he would pay him back as soon as he could. He hoped he would be able to pay him the following month. His father thought the following year was more probable, but gave him the money in the end.

(2) Anne told her husband, George, that they ought to have the sitting-room done up. The wallpaper was beginning to peel and the paint was scratched in some places where the children had been playing. George agreed that it looked a bit of a mess and said he would do the room up as soon as he had a weekend free. Anne said that she had not thought he would have time to do it himself. She added that he always lost his temper if things went wrong. Perhaps it would be better to leave the job to someone else. George thought she meant that he was

not capable of decorating the room himself but she said that was not true. Her reason for saying it was that she hated to see him working at the weekend when he was tired. Then George admitted that he *had* been feeling rather tired. Anne took advantage of this to say she was glad he agreed with her. She had already enquired at a shop in Market Street and they had quoted a very reasonable price. She would tell them to come round the following week to do the job.

(3) Clive Wells, a television interviewer, welcomed viewers to his programme and then introduced his guest, James Stanford. Stanford had been one of the country's leading Shakespearian actors for many years. However, it appeared that he had never made a film. Stanford corrected this impression. In fact, he had just finished making his first film, a spy picture. Wells asked him if he had found it difficult to get used to the new medium and Stanford replied that at first he had, because it is hard to act for a camera and technicians when one is used to a live audience. He compared it to being on television. Wells asked what the film was about. Was it a historical spy picture? Stanford said that for once he was playing a modern part, that of a counter-espionage agent. Wells wondered if he had had to disguise himself for the part. He supposed that Stanford must be used to wearing false beards and things like that in his Shakespearian roles. Stanford said he had only worn the usual make-up. For once the audience would be able to see his real face when the film came out. In conclusion, Wells asked him why he had made the extraordinary change from theatre to films and from Shakespeare to a modern spy drama. Stanford said he had done it for money, the same reason why he was appearing on Wells's programme.

B Reported Speech (2)

The main points of the first dialogue are reproduced

below in reported speech. Summarise Dialogues (2) and (3) in the same way in not more than 120 words. Do not try to include all the facts but choose those you would think sufficiently important to repeat to give someone else an idea of the conversation.

Tom asked his father to lend him five pounds because he wanted to buy a new shirt and tie for his girl-friend Janet's birthday party the following Saturday. When his father remarked that he had given him some money the week before, Tom explained that he needed that to buy Janet's present. As he was Janet's boy-friend, he would have to look smart. Mr Bradford did not think that Tom would pay him back for a long time but lent him the money in the end.

C   Composition

Write dialogues appropriate to the following situations.

(1) Two friends meet by accident at a station for the first time in many years.
(2) You have bought something from a shop and wish to exchange it.
(3) You are inviting a friend to a party at your house.
(4) You have just arrived in a town abroad on holiday and go to the Tourist Information Office to ask about the facilities it offers in order to decide whether to stay there.
(5) You would like to go to England to study English. You are trying to persuade your father to help pay for your studies there.
(6) Another driver has just driven into the back of your car while you are waiting at some traffic lights.

H

32 Explanation

(1) *Finding the Way*

3 Lincoln Court,
Pitt Road,
London W.19 8BN
29 May, 1973

Dear Heidi,

Fancy the two of us meeting by chance in London! I couldn't help wondering if it was really you when I saw you in Oxford Street. I hope you didn't mind me rushing
5 away but we'll have plenty of time to talk when you come to dinner on Thursday. I'm sure I gave you my address but I didn't tell you how to get here and so, as you're not on the 'phone, I thought the best thing to do would be to drop you a line.
10 You'll be coming into Charing Cross Station. That's the best line from where you're staying. From Charing Cross, you can either take the underground to Ealing Broadway or catch a 321 bus. The underground is much quicker, though you have a longer walk when you arrive.
15 It's no use mentioning taxis, of course. They cost the earth for a journey of six or seven miles. So take the District line from Charing Cross underground.

Remember that the underground station in the main station is Strand, not Charing Cross. When you come off
20 the platform, turn right down a flight of steps and right again down Villiers Street. Charing Cross underground station is straight ahead of you. Take the westbound train, not the eastbound, or you'll end up at the Tower of London!
25 There's only one exit at Ealing Broadway. You come out into the main road. Pitt Road is about a quarter of an hour's walk from there. Turn left down the main road, cross over at the traffic lights and go along Marshall Road. When you have crossed four or five
30 side-roads, you'll come to St Paul's Church. Turn right along Fox Road and you'll find that Pitt Road is the second on the left. Lincoln Court is set back from the

road on the left-hand side. There's a sign outside. Come
through the main door and my flat is straight in front of
35 you when you reach the top of the stairs on the first floor.

Richard and I are very much looking forward to seeing
you. Any time after six-thirty will suit us fine.

Affectionately,
Pamela

(2) *The NSPCC*

How does it come about that a society like the National
Society for the Prevention of Cruelty to Children is still
needed in a civilised country? At first sight, it may seem
strange that the Society, a voluntary organisation
5   which receives no financial help from the Government,
employs about 300 inspectors and deals with several
thousand cases every year.

When the Society was founded towards the end of the
nineteenth century its inspectors continually came across
10 cases of children who had been physically ill-treated.
One of the main reasons for this was drunkenness.
Alcohol was cheap and many fathers got drunk on their
way home after getting their weekly wages and hit their
wives and children.

15 Such cases are rare nowadays and improvements in
working conditions have ensured that few children are
hungry. The Society has far fewer cases to deal with in
proportion to the size of the population than before.
But it still comes up against new problems every day.

20 Most cases today are of neglect, rather than physical
cruelty. The parents have far more children than they
wanted and are too ignorant to look after them properly.
Although the state helps them with cheap rents and
allowances, they cannot organise their lives well enough
25 to use the money properly. Parents of neglected children
are often separated or divorced. Occasionally, they are
cruel by nature.

The Society's original task was to stop cruelty when it
was already taking place. The success of its work and its
30 value to the community is proved by the fact that its
main job now is educating people and trying to improve
home conditions so that cruelty and neglect do not start.

(3) *Computers*

Computers affect almost everyone in the modern world but most people either despise them or are afraid of them. Some think they are just enormous adding machines while others regard them as superhuman
5 electronic brains that will eventually dominate the human species. Neither of these ideas is correct.

A computer has the power to calculate at superhuman speed and so it can quickly solve problems that would take any human mathematician years of work. It has a
10 memory for storing information that is far more reliable than a human memory. But what matters most in a computer is its program.

Programming a computer for use in a factory, for example, may mean working out all the problems that
15 may come up in running it and the way to solve them. The programmer must foresee every imaginable combination of circumstances and give the machine appropriate instructions.

If the programmer knows the answers, why don't the
20 management ask him, instead of the computer? The answer is that conditions are constantly changing in a modern factory. If the computer is simultaneously connected to different processes it can warn management of trouble before it occurs. Sometimes a factory manager
25 can save a lot of money if he knows in advance what would be the most suitable time to close down for maintenance. In some cases, the factory is so complex that no individual can be aware of all the relevant facts at the same moment and so put something right that is
30 going wrong. The computer has the 'superhuman' capacity to solve problems like these but it can only give the right advice if the human programmer foresaw all the variables that might occur and included them in the program.

A Gerunds after Certain Phrases

Complete the sentences by using the gerund form of appropriate verbs.

(1) It's no use .... him. He doesn't know the answer.

(2) I was so surprised to see you that I couldn't help
.... if it was really you.

(3) Fancy the two of us .... by chance in Oxford Street!

(4) It's no good .... for a bus. The last one left half
an hour ago.

(5) Imagine him .... on the left-hand side of the road
in France and not .... it was wrong!

B Phrasal Verbs — Come

Complete the sentences with one of the following prepositions – *about, across, in for, off, on, out, out with, over,
round, up, up against*

(1) How does it come .... that we still need a society
like the NSPCC in a civilised country?

(2) At that time, inspectors continually came ....
children who had been ill-treated.

(3) A computer should be programmed to warn
management of problems as soon as they come .....

(4) Computers have come .... a lot of criticism from
people who do not really understand their purpose.

(5) I think she's fainted. Perhaps she'll come .... if
we throw water on her face.

(6) We tried various methods of solving problems
before installing the computer but none of them
came .....

(7) The NSPCC come .... new problems every day.

(8) Fancy him throwing his dinner on the floor! I
can't understand what came .... him for him to
do a thing like that.

(9) His new book has just come .... and the film
version of his last one is coming .... in London
next week.

(10) At first she was too upset to tell us what had happened but then she came .... it all at once.

C Composition

Here are some suggestions for compositions which involve
explanation. Answer them in about 150 words.

(1) Describe one of the ways in which a scientific

    invention or development has made life easier for housewives.

(2) Explain how any crop is grown and harvested in your country.

(3) Explain how advertising can be used to sell a product.

(4) What are the main forms of transport in town and country areas in your country?

(5) Explain the aims and intentions of any national or international charitable organisation.

(6) Explain the organisation of the processes needed to produce something in any factory you know.

(7) Explain how mechanical aids can make office work easier.

(8) You are going abroad on holiday with a friend who lives in a different town. Write a letter to him, arranging to meet him in a third place convenient to you both.

(9) What sort of domestic animal would you like to have as a pet? Give your reasons.

(10) Explain how children can be protected from common accidents in the home or in the streets.

33 Narrative

(1) *No Welcome at the Hotel*

I once had to go to a town in the north of England on business. My secretary went through the list of hotels in the Railway Guide to try to find one for me. The two that were recommended were both full and there was no
5 information to go on about the third. She took a chance and made the booking.

    It was half-past seven before I reached the hotel, which was in a quiet street opposite a church. The manageress was a stern old lady of about sixty. She showed me to my

10 room herself because there was no porter and when I
asked her about dinner, she said there was only one
sitting, at six-thirty, and I had missed it.

'Never mind,' I said amiably. 'I'm not hungry. I'll just
have a drink in the bar and then go to a restaurant.'

15 'Bar!' she said, raising her eyebrows. 'This is a respect-
able hotel, young man. If you want alcohol you must go
somewhere else.' She spoke as if a glass of beer were a
dangerous drug.

I had dinner and noticed that there was a good film at
20 the local cinema. When I returned to the hotel it was
half-past eleven. Everything was in darkness. I banged
on the door but nothing happened. The only sound was
the church clock opposite, which suddenly struck the
half hour with such force that it made me jump. Eventually
25 a window opened upstairs and the old lady looked out.
'What's going on?' she asked. I made her understand
who I was and she let me in after ten minutes' wait.
She was in her nightdress and her hair was in curlers.
'Guests are to be back in the hotel by eleven o'clock,' she said. 'The
30 same rule goes for everyone.'

I went to my room and tried to sleep. The bed was hard
and the sheets and blankets were damp. Every quarter of
an hour the church clock struck and at midnight the whole
hotel shook with the noise. Just before dawn, I finally
35 got off to sleep.

When I arrived at breakfast, everyone else had nearly
finished and there was not enough coffee to go round.

'Did you have a comfortable night's rest, young man?'
the old lady asked.

40 'To tell the truth, I don't think I could go through another
night in that room,' I replied. 'I hardly slept at all.'

'That's because you were up all night drinking alcohol!'
she said disapprovingly, putting an end to the conversation.

(2) *Too Late for the Wedding*
A year or so ago a close friend of mine, Ian Morris,
decided to get married and invited me to the wedding.
Of course I accepted but then found out that Ian's
fiancée, Virginia, came from a little village in the Welsh

5   mountains and *the wedding was to be held at the village church.*
Ian's own family would need all the beds at Virginia's
parents' house and the local inn but the couple had
arranged the wedding for the afternoon to give everyone
time to get there. I was to travel up with another friend,
10 Bill Stewart.

Bill went in for physical training and mountaineering
but I was still a bit surprised to see him dressed only in a
pair of shorts when he came to pick me up. It was such a
hot day that he did not feel like driving in his best suit.
15 'We'll have lunch somewhere and I'll change then,'
he explained.

We were already twenty miles up the M1 when Bill
suddenly remembered that he had left the wedding
present he had bought at home. That was the beginning
20 of a chapter of accidents. First, we had to go back and get
the present. Then we were held up for a long time near
Birmingham because of a road accident in front of us.
I wanted to drive on to Wales but Bill insisted on stopping
for lunch. 'It's not good for your health to go without
25 food at the proper time,' he said firmly. Then he took
another quarter of an hour to get dressed for the wedding.

We were only ten miles away from the village and there
was still half an hour left before the wedding was to begin
when we found ourselves behind a giant tanker on a
30 mountain road. Bill hooted at it for miles but the driver
was deaf. Eventually, we got past. 'Come on, Bill,' I
shouted. 'At least we'll see them come out of the church.'
At that moment there was a loud bang and a hissing noise
and the car nearly went off the road. We had a puncture
35 and had to stop to fit the spare tyre.

When we arrived, there were still a few people left at
the reception. 'The wedding was a great success,' Virginia's father said. 'It went off splendidly. A pity you missed
it! Ian and Virginia went off on their honeymoon half
40 an hour ago. Still, there's a little champagne left. At
least that hasn't gone off.'

A   Be To

(1) *Guests are to be back in the hotel by eleven o'clock*

This sentence could be rewritten:

'Guests must be back in the hotel by eleven o'clock'

Use the correct tense of the verb *be* with *to* in place of the words in italic type in the following sentences.

    (a) This notice *must not be* taken away.

    (b) You *must* report to the Commanding Officer.

    (c) This exit *must* only *be* used in case of emergency.

    (d) The pilot told us that we *were not allowed to* remove our safety-belts until he gave us permission.

    (e) The captain told the soldiers that they *must not* leave their posts, whatever happened.

(2) *The wedding was to be held at the village church*

This sentence could be rewritten:

'The wedding was going to be held at the village church'

Use the correct tense of the verb *be* with *to* in place of the words in italic type in the following sentences.

    (a) There was still half an hour left before the wedding *was due to* begin.

    (b) *It had been arranged that* I *would* travel with Bill Stewart.

    (c) The happy couple *have arranged to* spend their honeymoon in Holland.

    (d) *It has been decided that* we *should* meet at John's house at eight o'clock.

    (e) The reception *is going to* take place at the Alhambra Hotel.

B   Phrasal Verbs — Go

Complete the sentences with one of the following prepositions – *about, back on, for, in for, off* (2), *on* (4), *round, through, through with, with, without* (2)

    (1) The police had no information to go....so they could not arrest him.

    (2) The old lady opened the window and asked what was going....

    (3) The same rule goes....everyone in this hotel.

    (4) I don't think I could go....another night in that bedroom.

(5) It's not good for your health to go....food at the proper time.
(6) The wedding went....splendidly.
(7) This milk has gone....We'll have to throw it away.
(8) That's not the way to go....the job. Let me show you how to do it.
(9) I'm going....the Cambridge examination this summer.
(10) He went....working although he was tired.
(11) He congratulated the bride and bridegroom and then went....to thank the guests for coming.
(12) There wasn't enough coffee to go....so I had to go....
(13) You shouldn't have gone....your promise.
(14) I was pleased that Ian and Virginia had finally decided to go....their wedding after being engaged for so long.
(15) That tie goes beautifully....your suit.

C   Composition

Describe what happened and what you did in the following situations. Write 150 – 200 words.

(1) You arrived in a strange town and could not find a hotel.
(2) You saw a road accident.
(3) You were in a lift between floors when it broke down.
(4) You ate a meal in a restaurant and then discovered that you had no money.
(5) You had a strange dream.
(6) You saw someone in the sea or a river shouting for help.

34 Description

(1) *An Old Friend*

I was looking forward to meeting my friend Keith again.
When he had written to me to say that he was coming to
Europe on business, I had promised to meet him at the
airport. It never entered my head that I might not
5 recognise him after twenty years. I still kept a clear picture
in my mind of a tall, athletic-looking fellow, with clear,
blue eyes and fair, curly hair – in short, a typical, bronzed
Australian.

The arrival of Keith's flight was announced. I waited
10 outside the customs hall as the passengers went by –
businessmen in smart suits with brief-cases full of papers,
flustered mothers with children holding their hands and
hanging on to their skirts, two air hostesses in neat
uniforms, a man with a wooden leg, leaning on a stick,
15 young people with long hair, dressed in jeans and shirts,
the boys with beards that showed the difference between
them. There was no sign of Keith.

I went to the entrance of the customs hall and looked
inside. The only person there, apart from the customs
20 officers, was a big man of about fifty wearing dark glasses,
with a bald head and a moustache. He came towards me
and stopped in front of me. Then he said in a flat, direct
voice that I would have recognised anywhere: 'You must
be Geoffrey. How you've changed! It must be this lousy
25 climate you have here in England.'

(2) *My Neighbours*

My next-door neighbours are a middle-aged couple.
The husband, Bert, is a big, broad-shouldered, round-
faced man who works in the local brewery. In most
families it is the wife who has the reputation for gossiping
5 but Bert is an exception. He is always happy to stop working in his front garden and talk to anyone who comes by,
especially children. Bert's ambition is to retire to the
country and buy a little pub. I am sure he would be an

ideal landlord. His old-fashioned hospitality would per-
10   suade anyone to stop to have another drink.

Doris, his wife, must be about the same age as he is, but
she is already white-haired. She is not a bit like him to look
at. She is thin and sharp-featured, but also a woman of
great intelligence. Bert once told me with a smile that
15   Doris was the brains of the family. 'If we ever buy that
pub, my wife will have to keep an eye on me and do the
accounts. I'm much too big-hearted. I'd buy the customers
drinks and we'd soon be out of business. But Doris is
clear-headed enough for both of us. That's why we're
20   such a good combination.'

(3)   *A Stolen Car*

My car was stolen the other day and the police asked me
to write down a description of it to help them trace the
thief. I was surprised that it had been taken because there
were plenty of faster, more up-to-date models in the
5   street but perhaps I was the only person foolish enough to
leave my door unlocked. I wrote the following description:
'My car is a standard 1965 Mini, painted red, number
ABC 456C. It is in good condition, except that there is a
lot of play in the steering. In fact, I was on my way to the
10   garage to have the steering adjusted when the car was
stolen. The only accessories are the seat belts, also of
standard make and design. The only distinguishing mark
that would help you is a scratch on the paintwork about
three inches long just above the left rear wheel. The
15   door on the passenger's side sticks and does not open
properly. But no doubt the thieves will spray it some other
colour and change the number plates!'

The police reported the next day that they had found
the car in a side-street three or four miles away. It was not
20   damaged but someone had stuck a note to the windscreen.
It read: 'To the owner. If you want to kill yourself with
this steering, go ahead. I've got better things to do.'

A   Prepositions used in Describing People and their Clothes

Complete the sentences with one of the following prepositions – *in, of, with.*

(1) The man....the dark suit came towards me.
(2) The air hostesses were dressed....blue.
(3) He looked at me....a serious expression.
(4) A young man....about twenty....curly hair came out of the customs hall.
(5) He is a person....considerable ability.
(6) A boy....jeans....a long beard knocked at the door.
(7) He is a man....good character,....broad shoulders, a round face and an amiable expression.
(8) The postman approached me....some letters in his hand.

B Adjectival -ed Forms

The adjective *round-faced* means 'with a round face'. *Broad-shouldered* means 'with broad shoulders'. Make similar adjectival formations from the following and join them to the nouns.

(1) A man with a bald head.
(2) A fellow with blue eyes.
(3) A woman with white hair.
(4) A woman with a clear head.
(5) A girl with sharp features.
(6) A man with a big heart.
(7) A man with a flat voice.
(8) A child with curly hair.
(9) A couple in middle age. (not usual in this form)
(10) A businessman with a bad temper.
(11) Hospitality in the old fashion. (not usual in this form)
(12) A soldier in a red coat.
(13) A car with three wheels.
(14) A book with thumb marks.
(15) A toy with a plastic cover.

C Composition

(1) Write descriptions of the following:
  (a) Your best friend.
  (b) A member of your family.

    (c) A character in a novel you have read.

    (d) A famous actor or actress.

    (e) Your next-door neighbours.

    (f) Your boss.

(2) (a) You met a friend for the first time in ten years. Describe the changes in his/her appearance.

    (b) You have to meet a client of your firm at the airport. Write a description of yourself and the clothes you will be wearing so that he will be able to identify you.

    (c) Describe how the bride, bridegroom, bridesmaids, etc. were dressed at a wedding you went to.

    (d) Describe how people dress for any traditional festival or celebration in your country.

(3) Write descriptions of the following:-

    (a) Your car or the car you would like to own.

    (b) Your room at home and any changes you would like to make to improve it.

    (c) An important building or monument in your country.

    (d) A domestic animal you have had as a pet.

    (e) A busy airport or railway station.

35 Descriptive Narrative

(1) *The First Scene of 'Hamlet'*

It is night in the castle of Elsinore in Denmark. A sentry is on guard and another one, Bernardo, comes to take his place. Both men are nervous and on edge, as if they expect something terrible to happen. Soon afterwards,
5 Marcellus, an officer, arrives on the scene with a gentleman called Horatio. The soldiers begin to tell Horatio about a strange vision they have seen on two previous

occasions. Horatio is a realist and does not believe in ghosts but while they are talking the figure of a ghost suddenly appears, dressed like the dead king of Denmark. Everyone is frightened but Horatio speaks to it. It does not answer him, apparently angry at his tone of voice. When it has gone, Horatio admits that the figure was just like the King. Everyone feels sure that this means that some important event is going to take place in Denmark. The ghost returns and Horatio begs it to tell them what it wants. It is on the point of speaking when a cock crows. It is dawn and the ghost disappears. The men are not surprised, since they believe that ghosts can only appear at night and that at Christmas the cock crows all night long and evil spirits are never seen. They decide to tell Prince Hamlet, the son of the dead king, what they have seen.

(2) *Popular Heroes*

Thousands of fans are here at the city airport today to welcome the famous pop group, Gorilla and the Ape Men, who have just returned from a triumphant tour of the United States. At this moment, I can see Gorilla himself, followed by the rest of the Ape Men, coming down the steps leading out of the plane and waving to the crowd. I feel sure Gorilla's parents, Mr and Mrs Albert Nutt, who are in the crowd, must be proud of their son today. They are not the only ones. I have heard that the group's efforts for the export trade will probably be recognised in the New Year's Honours List and Gorilla is to be invited to perform at Buckingham Palace.

Now a woman has broken through the police barrier. I'm sure I recognise the homely figure of Gorilla's mother, Mrs Hazel Nutt. This seems to be the signal for everyone to run towards the aircraft. What an extraordinary display of public affection! I have never seen such incredible scenes.

The Ape Men don't seem to know what to do. Gorilla is scratching his head. And now they are all running back inside the plane. Clearly the warmth of their welcome has been too much for these shy young lads.

Now the fans are trying to climb up the steps to reach

their heroes. They are breaking the windows . . . I regret
25   that I must now return listeners to our studio.

A   Telling the Story of a Book, Play or Film

In the following exercises, retell the story in the present
tense. Do not look at the text until you have finished.

(1) *The First Scene of 'Hamlet'*
It was night in the castle of Elsinore in Denmark. A
sentry was on guard, and another one, Bernardo, came to
take his place. Both men were nervous and on edge, as if
they expected something terrible to happen. Soon
afterwards, Marcellus, an officer, arrived on the scene
with a gentleman called Horatio. The soldiers began to
tell Horatio about a strange vision they had seen on two
previous occasions. Horatio was a realist and did not
believe in ghosts, but while they were talking, the figure
of a ghost suddenly appeared, dressed like the dead
king of Denmark. Everyone was frightened but Horatio
spoke to it. It did not answer him, apparently angry at his
tone of voice. When it had gone, Horatio admitted that
the figure had been just like the king. Everyone felt sure
that this meant that something important was going to
take place in Denmark. The ghost returned and Horatio
begged it to tell them what it wanted. It was on the point
of speaking when a cock crowed. It was dawn and the
ghost disappeared. The men were not surprised, since they
believed that ghosts could only appear at night and that at
Christmas the cock crowed all night long and evil
spirits were never seen. They decided to tell Prince Hamlet, the son of the dead king, what they had seen.

(2) *Pip and the Convict*
Pip was an orphan who lived with his sister and her
husband, Joe, near the Thames estuary. Joe was a blacksmith. The story took place early in the nineteenth
century when convicts were often confined in prison ships
on the river. One day Pip was visiting his parents' grave
when a man with a terrible expression suddenly appeared.
Pip noticed that he was wearing an iron on his leg and

realised that he was an escaped convict. The man told Pip to get him some food and a file so that he could take the iron off. He threatened to kill Pip if he did not bring the food or if he told anyone what he had seen. The little boy went home and stole the food from his sister's cupboard and the file from the blacksmith. The next morning, as early as he could, he went to find the convict and gave him what he had asked for. Although he was terrified, he could not help feeling sorry for the man. But he had no idea that one day the convict would become a rich man and remember his kindness.

B   Describing an Incident as it Happens

In the following exercises, imagine that you were present and that you were broadcasting what was happening to listeners on the radio. Write what you would actually have said. Do not look at the text at the beginning of the lesson until you have finished.

(1) *Popular Heroes*
Thousands of fans were at the city airport to welcome a famous pop group, Gorilla and the Ape Men, who had just returned from a triumphant tour of the United States. A radio commentator described the scene as Gorilla, followed by the rest of the Ape Men, came down the steps leading out of the plane and waved to the crowd. The commentator felt sure that Gorilla's parents, Mr and Mrs Albert Nutt, who were in the crowd, must be proud of their son. He thought they were not the only people who felt proud. He had heard that the group's efforts for the export trade would probably be recognised in the next New Year's Honours List and that Gorilla was to be invited to perform at Buckingham Palace.

Suddenly a woman broke through the police barrier. It was Gorilla's mother, Mrs Hazel Nutt, a homely figure. This was the signal for everyone to run towards the aircraft. The commentator was astonished at such an extraordinary demonstration of public affection and said he had never seen such incredible scenes before.

The Ape Men did not seem to know what to do.

Gorilla was scratching his head. Suddenly they all ran back inside the plane. The commentator remarked that the warmth of their welcome had clearly been too much for such shy young lads.

As the fans tried to climb up the steps to reach their heroes and began breaking the windows of the plane, the commentator quickly broke off the transmission and returned listeners to the studio.

(2) *A Famous Match*

The commentator was watching the World Cup football final between England and West Germany. It seemed certain that England would win. There was only a minute left and England were leading by two goals to one. The German team had scored first but England had soon equalised and a quarter of an hour later, Peters had given them the lead. At that moment, play was in the English half of the field and the referee had just blown his whistle. He awarded a free kick to Germany about forty yards from the English goal. All the players gathered in front of the goal. Only a few seconds remained. The kick was taken and the ball went up to the left of the English penalty area. Everyone was fighting for it. It flew across the face of the goal. The defenders could not get it away. Suddenly, Weber, the German left half, had the ball at his feet. Banks, the English goalkeeper, rushed to the other end of the goal to cover Weber's shot but it was too late. The ball was in the net. West Germany had levelled the score. The referee blew his whistle again to indicate the end of the normal period of play. The two teams would have to play extra time to decide who won the cup.

C   Composition

(1) Describe an incident in any novel you have read.
(2) Describe a scene in a play you have seen.
(3) Briefly tell the story of any film you have seen recently.
(4) You are at an airport broadcasting a description of

the arrival of a famous person. Write what you say
to the listeners.

(5) You are present at a sporting event. Describe the
scene to listeners on the radio.

(6) You are present at a traditional festival in your
country. Describe the scene in the streets as if you
were broadcasting over the radio.

Index

L

Large number of, A: 16C
Lay: 9F
Lend: 11E
Let: 5D
Let's: 12E
Letters: more formal 30; personal 29
Lie: 9F
Like: and *as* 3E, 8E; and *similar to* 18D
Little and *a little*: 16C
Look: phrasal verbs with 8F
Look forward to: 1E
Lot of, A: 16C

M

Make: and *do*, 27E; and *let* 5D; phrasal verbs with 30A
May: permission 11C; possibility 12C
Meet: 12F
Might: permission 11C; possibility 12C
More: 24D
More formal letters: 30
Most: 24D
Must: logical 13C; obligation and prohibition 13C

N

Narrative: 33
Needn't: 13C
No: and *not any* 16C
Not any: 16C
Not . . . any more: 10G
Noun clauses: 25C
Noun groups: 17E
Nouns: and articles 13D; used to represent classes, types and species 18F

O

On one's own: 17D

Q

Question tags: 14D
Question words: 14C
Quite: 2D

R

Raise: 7F
Rather: 2D
Reach: 7G
Relative adverbs: 23E
Relative clauses: co-ordinate 23D; defining 23C;
    non-defining 24C; participles as alternatives to 28E
Remember: 5E
Remind: 5E
Reported speech: into direct speech 31A; summarizing
    into 31B
Result, adverbial clauses of: 26C
Rise: 7F
Run: phrasal verbs with 23F

S

Say: 17F
See: phrasal verbs with 23G
Self: 29C
Set: phrasal verbs with 22F
Shall I?: 11C
Shall we?: 12E
Should: 13C
Similar to: 18D
Since: with *for* and *ago* 4D
Some: and *others* 16C
Stand: phrasal verbs with 5F
Still: 10G

T

U

V

W